BE THE G.O.A.T.

TALES OF A FUTURE CHAMPION

MICHAEL LANGDON DANIEL CLARK
MATTHEW HAMM

THIS BOOK BELONGS TO:

....

For Keith and Tony for taking us to our first ever soccer matches and starting our love of the game.
Ferdie, your grit and strength inspire me every day.

"You have to fight to reach your dream. You have to sacrifice and work hard for it."

LIONEL MESSI

CHAPTER 1

"MOM! WHAT'S TAKING YOU SO LONG?!" I SHOUT FROM the drive as I make my way to the car.

I swear this is payback for all the times I've kept *her* waiting on our way to school. But she should know it's important not to be late today. It's State Championship final day and we're facing our arch-rivals (and neighbors!) AFC City.

As I sit in the car for what seems like an eternity, I can't help but feel butterflies in my stomach. It's eight months since the season started and it comes down to one game. Sure, we won the league by a country mile, but this is the trophy that *really* matters.

The winners of this tournament will go on to represent the country at international level in the summer, and be invited by none other than the legendary Claudius Reyner to be coached in his academy. That's right, *the* Claudius Reyner - the greatest soccer player this country has ever produced.

"Have you got your soccer cleats, shin pads and water?" Mom asks as she finally jumps in the car.

"Yeah, you know I packed them last night, Mom", I reply.

"Remember honey, it's all about just enjoying yourself out there today."

I give her a warm smile, mostly to avoid any sort of disagreement. The reality is that it's *not* about that.

Yes, I will no doubt enjoy myself as I score a few goals, but today is *all* about winning!

⚽⚽⚽

With only a few minutes remaining, I can see the boys are starting to really enjoy themselves on the field (maybe Mom *was* right after all!). We're passing the ball around effortlessly and the opposition can't even get close to us!

I got two goals before half-time and two shortly after. We're comfortably leading 4-0, and with only a few minutes left on the clock, the opposition appear to have finally given up. The excitement around our team is palpable as we knock the ball around from wing to wing easily. I can see that even the boys on the bench are already giddy with excitement!

The ball makes its way to the feet of our winger Gus and I spot him quickly looking up to see who's in the box. I like playing with Gus, it feels like we can telepathically communicate. I'm standing by the penalty spot and want the ball played into the 6-yard box so I can head it in. I know that just by *looking* at Gus he's going to put the ball where I want it, so I start my run into the box.

Our telepathic communication has worked – Gus has indeed pinged a ball to the area – but his accuracy is not what I expected. As I start my run to the box, I see the ball is actually going to land slightly behind me. However, that doesn't *really* matter. Before I even realize what I'm doing, I fling myself in the air, with my back to goal, and bicycle kick the ball into the net.

The ball makes contact with my shin but rockets into the top right corner. WOW! What a goal! Even I have to admit that (and I'm usually quite critical of any goal I score!)

As I land on the floor with a thud, all 10 of my teammates rush over to celebrate with me. I hear the referee blow the full-time whistle in the background, and just like that, we are Champions!

5-0 and I scored all five of them! This really is *the* happiest day of my life!

After lifting the cup and celebrating with my teammates, I head over to Mom who is deep in conversation with two men dressed in gray suits. They look identical as they flank her on either side.

I know we've got to head straight to the airport after this to meet my sister and dad as we're going on holiday, so perhaps they are the drivers taking us there?

"Honey, you've got two gentlemen who have come to see you," Mom says.

"They both want to invite you to their elite soccer academy this summer to play for them. Gary represents the Claudius Reyner Academy," Mom says as she turns and gestures to her right. "Ramon here is from Argentina. He represents the prestigious Jewels Old Boys Academy in Buenos Aires."

"Honey, I hate to do this to you, but you have to make a decision now as we're running late to meet your dad and sister at the airport".

. . .

DECISION TIME

If you decide to go and play for Jewels Old Boys Academy in Buenos Aires, go to page 123

If you decide to go play for the Claudius Reyner Academy, go to page 141

CHAPTER 2

RING RING. RING RING. My phone vibrated in my pocket.

'Gus' cried my phone screen. "Hey man. What's up?" I answer, glad to hear a friendly voice from back home.

"Yo bro. Have you seen your name's trending?" he laughed excitedly.

"No, what do you mean? What's it about?" Fear and excitement crept into my voice.

"Bro, it's saying Manchester Devils are interested in you. They want to make a bid. MANCHESTER... BRO. MANCHESTERRRRRR!"

Wow. I wasn't ready for that news. Such an iconic club, so many trophies.

"But that's just rumors though? That doesn't mean it's true...right?" I asked.

"I dunno bro...there's literally thousands of posts about it." I could tell he was excited. "Someone has put you in the Manchester home jersey! It has 50,000 likes," he added before ending the call.

MANCHESTER. My brain was racing. I needed to speak to my agent…

RING RING. RING RING. RING RING.

No way, he was already calling me! Maybe the rumors were true.

"I was literally just about to call you. Everything okay?" I asked, pretending I didn't know that my name was trending…or had even heard of Manchester.

"Yeah great. We need to talk right away – are you home?"

He wasn't waiting around for pleasantries, this was serious.

"I'm home right now. What's up?" I started putting my shoes on, having a feeling I might need to be on the road quickly. I had a spidey-sense for these kinds of things.

"The London Lilywhites chairwoman wants to speak to you right away. We can meet her at her house. I think we're about to be offered a new contract and that number 10 jersey you've always wanted!"

This was the second time today I was hit with unexpected great news. Maybe I should buy a lottery ticket later.

"Wow. Are you serious? That's amazing!" It was as well, I loved this club. "…but can I ask about Manchester Devils – are the rumors true?" I asked, no longer playing it cool.

There were a few seconds of silence on the phone.

"Ah right, you mean the fact your name is trending. Yeah, I was hoping you hadn't seen that." I thought he would have been more excited.

"Well, despite the noise and rumors, Manchester Devils haven't made an official approach, but my contact says there is some interest in you. Having said that, they don't think the Lilywhites will let you go," he said, somewhat popping my Manchester balloon.

I stared out the window, trying to remind myself that a new contract here was great news... it just wasn't the famous Manchester Devils.

"This kind of stuff happens all the time, try and ignore the noise – the Lilywhites want to keep you and the fans sing your name every game," he said, trying to make me focus. "Stay at the club, become a legend. I really think with you staying they have a great chance to win a proper trophy."

"Yeah, it's great, I know. Sorry," I said, taking the Manchester jersey off in my head and throwing it onto the fire. "What time does she want me there?"

"In an hour – meet you there?" He hung up, leaving me with my thoughts.

⚽ ⚽ ⚽

I got to the house a few minutes early. My mom always said, being early is being on time. The house was HUGE, more like a castle. It had two turrets, a moat and a bright pink army tank outside. The chairwoman wasn't known for keeping her head down.

As I pulled up to the house, she walked confidently through the large wooden front doors and waved at me, holding what must be the contract in her hand. This wasn't going to take long.

"Here he is. The man of the hour. My new number 10." She flashed a set of bright white teeth.

Behind her, my agent appeared, scuttling along like a hungry rat with cheese in his sights.

"I know number 10 will look good on you, son. Do you know who last wore that number at the club?" He beamed, laughing at me.

I knew. Everyone knew. The greatest attacking midfielder in London Lilywhites history. I secretly gulped.

"Sorry, could I have a quick word with the kid please?" My agent said, steering me away from the grinning chairwoman.

"Good to see you mate. We need to have a quick chat before we walk into the lioness' den." I was confused, he seemed so keen about this contract earlier.

"Sooooo Manchester..." he whispered to me.

"I have some news. My contact tells me if you were to force a move from Lilywhites, they would be open to making an official offer."

I froze. He was asking me to do something I was uncomfortable with. Annoy the club enough that they have no option but to sell me.

"I mean...that's great news." It was. "...but I can't do that to the club, to the chairwoman, to the fans. They'll hate me. It'll ruin my legacy here."

He waited a beat and smiled at me. "That's the game kid."

Some of the greats have had to make tough decisions, often turning their backs on a club to take a step up. Question is, which career do you want?"

DECISION TIME

If you accept the chairwoman's offer, go to page 58

If you try and persuade the chairwoman to sell you to Manchester, go to page 118

If you try and force the move to Manchester by driving to their training ground, go to page 121

CHAPTER 3

WITH A LONG-TERM CONTRACT SIGNED, I STARTED TO settle into life in Germany. We missed out on silverware that season, but over the next four years we shared two league titles apiece with Bayer Monchen. Those were great days at Westfalen, and I broke the records for individual goals and assists at the club three times. We reached three European Cup semifinals and lost narrowly to FC Catalonia, a Zhivec-inspired Milano, and our rivals, Bayer. Whilst we never quite got over the line to reach a European final, the domestic cup proved more fruitful, and we won it three times over five years.

I was settled here, and I could now afford to fly my family out regularly, so homesickness no longer bothered me as much.

In the final year of my contract, offers came in from all over the world, including lucrative offers from Saudi Arabia and China. However, only two offers were enough to make me consider moving. They came from FC Catalonia and Manchester

Devils, two of the biggest clubs in the world who regularly won European trophies and domestic titles.

My agent, who would receive a large percentage fee if I moved, was keen for me to speak with FC Catalonia and Manchester. But there was also a contract offer on the table from Westfalen, the club to which I owed so much of my success.

DECISION TIME

To sign for FC Catalonia, go to page 136

To sign a new contract at Westfalen, go to page 51

CHAPTER 4

"YOU KNOW WHAT GUS, I THINK I'LL PASS, MAYBE YOU should think about laying off the nights out as well for a bit? Your recent performances haven't been as good as I know they could be."

Gus looks a little offended for a moment then just laughs, his usually relaxed expression returning to his face "Suit yourself bro, but don't train too hard!" and with that he's gone.

My teammates keep acting the same for the remainder of the week - leaving training as soon as they can to go out partying. Meanwhile, I choose to stay behind practicing free kicks over and over again, left side, right side, central.

I do this over and over again, refusing to go home until I hit 15 *perfect* free kicks in a row. One night I didn't get home until dark but it always feels worth it, it always feels like I'm improving. Bring on the cup game at the weekend!

⚽ ⚽ ⚽

It's 3-3 with minutes left to play, we beat this team easily earlier in the season. Needless to say, it's been a below-par performance from everyone. Everyone that is, except *me*. I scored a penalty that I won myself, scored a long range left footed finish and a solo goal where I dribbled through their defense and chipped the goalkeeper. That extra training has really been paying off.

As the clock ticks down, Gus breaks through their defense cutting in from the right wing. I peel off into space calling for the ball waiting for the pass, a simple squared ball and I've got an easy finish to win it! Gus delays, takes too long to make the pass and the recovering defender clatters through him taking him out before getting to the ball.

Peeeep the referee signals a free kick to us. It's just outside the box, right-hand side, a little close perhaps to get up and over the wall, but a great position for a left footed player like myself. I walk over to place the ball as Gus puts his arm around me "I know you've seen the scout in the crowd from FC Catalonia bro - make this count, yeah?"

I clock the scout again, just like I have done every time I've scored today. The FC Catalonia badge gleams on his training top. The badge on the iPad he keeps making notes on is a clear giveaway as to what he's doing here. I pick the ball up and kiss it before placing it back down. I look at Gus, "Don't worry pal, I've got this."

I take my usual three steps back from the ball and three to the side, I breathe deep and compose myself, just like I have done over and over again in training. All those hours, all those shots, *all* for this moment.

I notice a slight gap in the wall, a smaller player

between two taller ones, if I can just get in up and over that gap with a bit of curl I could find the top corner of the goal.

I start my run up, and then connect sweetly with my instep – just below the valve of the ball, sending it up through the wall and down again in a flash. It nestles in the top corner of the goal. All before the goalkeeper has even *moved*!

What. A. Goal!

⚽ ⚽ ⚽

The final whistle blows with the game ending 4-3 and I'm mobbed by my teammates. Despite the initial happiness, all I'm now interested in is finding out about the scout from FC Catalonia.

As the celebrations start to die down and I walk back to the locker rooms with my head held high, I find the scout talking to my manager before he turns to talk to me:

"You did yourself proud out there today, if only every young player had your level of application and hard work. You've got the skill for sure, but it's your determination that really sets you apart."

He pauses for a moment.

"We want you to come and join us in Spain. Congratulations buddy, you're going to the big leagues!"

Go to page 18

CHAPTER 5

It wasn't hard getting FC Catalonia to see me play. It turns out my cousin, Albe, had a family friend who was a scout for FC Catalonia, and he agreed to see me play the weekend after I landed in Spain!

I never knew professional soccer contracts could be signed on napkins, but after that first game when I had scored eight goals, Charlie Rex (the FC Catalonia scout) took me and my dad for lunch, scribbled something on a napkin, and informed us that this would tie me to FC Catalonia for the next two years.

"Not until you write down that you'll pay for the growth hormone treatment," Dad said with his best poker face.

Rex didn't hesitate to add it to the napkin and handed it over to me and dad to sign. I quickly scribbled down my name and tucked into the gorgeous paella Rex had ordered for the table.

⚽ ⚽ ⚽

Eight months had passed since that first weekend in Spain. And it had been a pretty rough time.

My sister and mom left Spain after two months of being here. My mom hated the weather, and my sister was being bullied at school. They were both crying every day so they flew back home whilst dad and I stayed here to see if FC Catalonia would offer me a professional contract.

To add insult to injury, Jewels Old Boys were saying I couldn't play for FC Catalonia because technically I was still part of their team.

This would all be solved in a matter of months when my contract with them expired, but it meant that I had only been playing friendlies and non competitive matches. A friendly game just isn't the same! And they would only happen once a week or so. The rest of my time, I either spent it training by myself or crying because I missed my mom and sister.

Right now, however, I feel like I'm about to break through into the first team with FC Catalonia. I am also extremely grateful that the pills they have given me to help my growth seem to be working. I am perhaps a little shorter than everyone, but I still compete on every level.

Despite this, I often think about just going back home to reunite our family. I'm very conscious that my family has been divided because of their belief that I'll make it as a professional soccer player here in Spain.

DECISION TIME

If you miss your family too much and decide to permanently move back home, go to page 151

If you decide that missing your family for a little bit longer is worth it to try and become a professional soccer player, go to page 18

CHAPTER 6

THE FC CATALONIA MANAGER CALLED ME INTO HIS office:

"Young man, I think you're a diamond in the rough! However, I don't know if you've got the tenacity to become a professional player, you're way too quiet on the field!" He started to get a bit agitated, which is *never* a good sign from your boss!

"I like you but..."

Oh no, not a 'but' I thought, 'buts' are bad...

"... but you're just too shy and quiet. I need you to liven up around here! Act like you *want* to be here."

"I LOVE being here, boss!" I wanted to scream that out, but kept it to myself. Perhaps he *did* have a point about me being too quiet!

"Anyway, I've had enough of all the senior players nagging me to play you in the First Team. Apparently you've had a few friendlies with them and absolutely destroyed them in training. They *CANNOT* stop raving about you, and they *CANNOT* stop pestering me to play you in the First Team."

I suddenly felt a change of vibe...maybe this chat *wasn't* going to end badly after all.

"Make sure you have an early night on Friday, kiddo. You're starting in this Saturday's pre-season friendly against Valle Rayecano."

My heart skipped a couple of beats as my body froze.

"Thanks, boss". That's all I could muster. WOW, maybe he was right. Maybe I was too quiet!

I scored two goals in my first ever First Team game. Yeah, it was a friendly match, but I enjoyed what the press had printed about this new teenage wonder kid breaking onto the scene. Some reporters said that I was destined to be one of the 'World's Best.'

It felt good making my mom and sister proud. They were still back home in a different country, but they knew we had made the right decision as a family because we were *all* doing better.

⚽⚽⚽

It has been seven months since my debut game for the First Team and those two goals, but the manager hasn't given me another chance to play yet.

I have scored 27 goals and got 12 assists for the Second Team in the last seven months but the manager, for some reason, still doesn't think that's good enough to earn me a promotion to the First Team.

Apparently, I've still got a lot to learn as a young player, but I feel like I'm ready to play for them now!

I was starting to get very frustrated with this situation, when a scout for Westfalen in Germany suggested we meet. I am very new to this scene, but I know *exactly* what this means. The German giants are obviously interested in signing me. If I do meet up with him I'd have to sneakily do it behind FC Catalonia's back - they wouldn't be happy if they found out.

And, it turns out, agents are like city buses. You wait forever for one, and then two come along at the same time!

I've just been informed that the North London team, London Lillywhites, are interested in signing me as well. Their agent also wants to meet up with me.

Sure, London Lilywhites are not as big as Westfalen, but it could mean that I get more game time. And in England of all places! This is a tough decision for me...

DECISION TIME

To sneak off and meet up with the agent from Westfalen FC, go to page 56

To sneak off and meet up with the agent from London Lilywhites, go to page 181

To keep your head down and focus on your career with FC Catalonia, go to page 172

CHAPTER 7

I had been playing for Catalonia's first team for the last six months, and every morning I had to pinch myself to make sure I wasn't dreaming!

Sure, I was only playing the last 10 minutes or so of every match, but I was playing soccer every weekend with global superstars like Bobaldinho, Decu and Carlos Puñol. I was living the dream, and it could not get any better… or could it?

A couple of minutes after coming on against FC Malacete, I played a ball to Bobaldinho on the edge of the 18-yard box.

I instinctively kept running after passing the ball to him. More in hope than anything else, as I immediately saw that he was surrounded by a sea of Malacete players. Not surprising given that he was the best player on earth and could punish you from anywhere around the box.

I started to slow my run down as I knew it was impossible for Bobaldinho to get past the five players circling him. But then, out of nowhere, I see the ball being ballooned over the heads of the defenders and directly in front of me. Bobaldinho *really could* create something out of nothing.

I take a quick glance toward the keeper, who has started to dash towards the ball. I'm going to get to it first, but it's bouncing unpredictably; so with no other option, I gently lob it over the oncoming goal-keeper. He outstretches his fingertips as a last gasp effort to stop the ball, but he can only brush it as it floats into the back of the net.

I'm paralyzed! I have just scored my first goal for Catalonia and I've got Bobaldinho holding me aloft on his shoulders.

"Take it all in, brother!" He says proudly.

"This is surely the first of many!" He says as he happily drops me and my other teammates come in to join us.

Puñol gives me a gentle, playful slap in the face! "YES! WHAT A FINISH, LITTLE MAN," he says ecstatically. I know he means well and is happy, but wow that slap *really* hurt.

Ouch! As the melee from the celebration breaks up I feel like my hamstring is about to snap. I must have pulled it trying to make contact with the ball whilst it was so high up in the air.

Hobbling back to the center circle, Decu comes over and gently pats me on the head. "You've surely cemented your spot in the Champions League semi-final next week with that goal, little man".

Oh yeah! I had temporarily forgotten that the Champions League semi-final against London Blues was next week. What a bad time to pick up this small injury!

As the full-time whistle goes, the manager

approaches me offering his congratulations. "How are you feeling, Kiddo?"

Obviously I'm elated, but straight away I feel like I have a decision to make as to whether I should tell him about the niggle on my hamstring.

DECISION TIME

To try and help your team in the semi-final by keeping the hamstring niggle to yourself, go to page 98

To tell the manager that you have a slight hamstring niggle, go to page 179

CHAPTER 8

Winning the League Cup with London Lilywhites ended up being the only bit of silverware I won in England.

I had been at the club for 14 years, and we had only managed a couple of domestic finals and qualification for Europe a handful of times.

We also had some epic wins over our arch-rivals Gunnerbury in that time.

As the curtain went down on my final game for London Lilywhites, I couldn't help but feel enormous gratitude for my parents back home.

They had given everything for me to play abroad.

And considering I was just a small town boy who once had a soccer dream – the dream in the end became somewhat of a fairy tale.

And just like that my soccer career ended.

CHAPTER 9

KNOCK KNOCK KNOCK KNOCK KNOCK KNOCK!

I wake up from my deep sleep very alarmed as to who could be knocking on my door so urgently at this early hour.

It's my club teammate and fellow countryman, Jodier Mastichano, carrying seven newspapers under his arm.

"You've done it, my man! Let it sink in," he says excitedly.

"What are you on about?" I respond, half asleep, yawning.

Before you know it, he's laid out all the national newspapers on the breakfast table. The headlines make it clear that I've been called up to the national team to play in the upcoming World Cup in Germany.

I give Jodier a big hug and feel an incredible sense of pride and happiness, but it's whilst I'm looking over his shoulder at the headlines that the feeling suddenly changes.

I'm overwhelmed reading some of the papers and the things they are saying about me:

"He's carrying the hopes and dreams of 40 million of us."

"He's the savior of our national team."

"20 years of pain will be erased by him."

"He's the greatest teenager the world has ever seen."

Wowsers! Had they forgotten that soccer was a team sport?! That there were 10 other players on the field to help out?

Even the great Dogo Armenio Marantini was saying that I was his successor-in-waiting!

I knew I was meant to be happy, but reading these headlines suddenly put an awful lot of pressure on me. It made me feel very uncomfortable.

"It's time to warm up, son." I feel the adrenaline shoot through my veins as the manager says those words to me.

We're already 4-0 up against Slovakia, and there's 20 minutes left of the game. Forget about making my *debut* in a World Cup, I'm confident I can *score* on my debut. I smell blood. The Slovakians are tired and their heads are down.

Within seconds of coming on I make a run towards the edge of the box as Juan Remus Rocalme finds me with a perfectly weighted ball. Instinctively, I toe-poke it before the keeper can react and score my first goal for my national team. I look up at the adoring fans who are celebrating the 5th goal we've put past Slovakia - they are in heaven!

A few minutes later, I glide past a couple of Slovakians attempting to chop me down and play a through ball to Pauly Haima. He dinks over the keeper to make it 6-0. We have finally arrived in this tournament, and with a 6-0 scoreline it's clear to see we're favorites to win it.

⚽ ⚽ ⚽

The next day, the papers couldn't stop praising me

"He will single handedly bring the trophy home."

"No one like him since the biggest of them all: Dogo Armeni Marantini."

"The Boy Wonder has entered the world stage."

It really felt good to be helping the team out. That's why it came as a shock when the manager benched me for the next game against Ivory Coast. He didn't even bring me on. Perhaps he was resting me as we had already qualified for the next round? As much as it got to me, I decided not to bring it up with the manager, after all, he was in charge, and well… I was still only a young!

⚽ ⚽ ⚽

"What is wrong with the manager?!" There's 20,000 adoring fans chanting my name, urging him to bring me on, but he's still not budging!

We're 2-0 down against the Germans, and the home side are completely dominating the game.

If we beat them, we go through as group winners and take on the minnows of New Zealand. If we come second we'll face a strong France team.

I'm sure I can make a difference if he just brings

me on. There's 15 mins to go. Come on, boss. I am begging you to bring me on…

The Germans ended up scoring two more goals in those last 15 minutes and we lost the game 4-0.

As I trudged back to the dressing room, shoulders slumped, I noticed that my national team manager was right next to me. I feel a flurry of emotions, everything from sadness to anger.

Sadness because we'd made our journey harder for the one competition that I had wanted to win the most. I had been dreaming about lifting the World Cup since I was 4 years old and it was likely that we'd lose to the French.

Anger because the manager didn't play me at all against the Germans. I *know* I could have made a difference - I know I could have given us the easy path against New Zealand.

As we rub shoulders, I can't help but let my feelings get the better of me, and in an explosion of emotion I let the manager know how I'm feeling…

DECISION TIME

If you explode in a fit of anger and demand to know why you didn't play, go to page 157

If you tell the manager how upset you are and how it's only fueled your desire to work harder and train harder to be in the first 11 for the next game, go to page 136

CHAPTER 10

"I WANTED TO LET EVERYONE KNOW THAT THE LAST three weeks have been very tough for me and my family."

I was focused on staring at one bright light on top of a camera at the end of the room as I continued…

"...It's now time for everyone in the country, and especially the people in this room who are adding fuel to the fire, to stop it. Let's draw a line under this and focus on next year's Continental Championships."

⚽⚽⚽

A year had passed since that famous press conference and yet again we found ourselves in the final of the Continental Championships.

Fixture congestion had meant there were back-to-back Continental Championships followed by a winter World Cup In the United Arab Emirates. A never-before-seen congestion of international tournaments.

In that time, Portugal's Renato Conaldo had won a Continental Championship himself. That was only increasing my hunger to win something with my national team!

It had been 20 years since my debut with the national team and I had won no major honors. We'd lost so many finals that I felt like we were cursed. Especially after winning so many trophies with FC Catalonia and seven FISA 'Best Player in The World' awards.

I had two more 'Best Player in The World' awards than Conaldo did, but I knew that didn't matter for much. All that matters is winning something for your country...and he'd already done that!

⚽⚽⚽

We lined up under the Werberly arch once again in an international final. As captain, I looked across the young group of players who were under my guidance.

Some of them were still teenagers - they hadn't even been *born* when I made my debut for the national team - and here we were, together as one, trying to beat the Brazilians to bring the Continental Championship back to our people.

Our people had been through a lot and it had been *decades* since we had won anything on the international stage.

After we belted the national anthem to the top of our lungs, I instructed my teammates to form a huddle near the center circle.

As captain, I had to inspire this group of young boys to give it their all for this game. I didn't want them to go through what I had been through for the last 20 years. It was time we did ourselves proud and delivered!

"Boys, it's been 45 days since we've seen our families!" I shouted rousingly over the noise of the fans.

"Some of us have missed the birth of our children to be here! And you know what? It's because fate wanted it to be this way. Fate wanted us to win this trophy, right here, right now at Werberly, the home of soccer."

I don't know what was coming over me, but I was feeling pumped - *incredibly inspired*! The words kept coming out of my mouth and from my heart...

"...so I'm telling you now, pull your socks up and let's go out there and fight. Because this trophy comes home with us tonight!"

⚽ ⚽ ⚽

Sensing our attacking threat, the Brazilians were compact and defended well. They were happy to sit deep and absorb all our pressure in the first half, and in fairness to them they did well to shut us down.

A nondescript, and quite frankly boring first half finished 0-0.

There were now 10 minutes left of the game and the Brazilians were finally starting to attack us, freeing up space on the wings to attack. As the Brazilians were lining up to take a corner, I went over to my young teammate Alex McPallister, put my hand over my mouth and said:

"Listen, I need your pinpoint accuracy, brother. Their left-back is leaving so much space on the flank.

If you get the ball, just ping it there and I will find your pass. Trust me."

McPallister was only young, but I knew his passing was second to none. I don't know why, out of all the players on my team, I said this to McPallister. It was almost as if I knew in advance that the Brazilian's miskicked corner would end up at his feet. Lo and behold, it did, and I exploded into the fastest sprint of my life.

I ran into the space vacated by their defender on the left wing as McPalister pinged a beautifully lofted ball 30 yards just ahead of me. I was clearly onside and all I had to do was control the ball and beat the last defender.

It's now or never.

I brought the ball down with my right thigh and pushed it into my stride with my left foot. The defender in front of me was running backwards, jockeying my run, in the hope to buy some time for his teammates to arrive.

I dropped my right shoulder to feint going right before quickly changing direction and pushing the ball past the defender's left.

He collapsed, flat onto his bottom, as I went past him, I looked up to see the keeper coming off his line to try and stop me. He was quick to do so, and was only two or three yards away from me at this point.

I didn't want to wait. I didn't *have* to wait - Instinctively, I chipped the ball over him and it bounced into the back of the net.

Not breaking my stride I turned around to see all my teammates rushing towards me, arms outstretched. 30,000 roaring fans behind me and 10 young players rushing to celebrate with me.

This is what soccer was all about. As they clambered upon me I took it all in. What a time to be alive. But I quickly had to get over the undiluted joy.

"It's not over lads." We've got 10 more minutes to go.

⚽ ⚽ ⚽

We fought like warriors for the last 10 minutes, bravely withstanding a barrage of fierce Brazilian attacks.

When the full-time whistle went there was a field invasion. The backroom staff, all the unused substitutes and all my teammates on the field rushed to be with me. We had done it! We had brought the Continental Cup back home.

"CHAMPIONE, CHAMPIONE, OLE, OLE OLE!"

We all sang to the top of our lungs in a huge circle in front of our fans. Everywhere you looked there was champagne popping and people smiling from ear to ear.

I had finally done it, I had finally won a major international tournament for my country.

⚽ ⚽ ⚽

Winning the Continental Championship was great. It gave the whole team belief that we could potentially win the most elusive of *all* sports trophies; THE BIG ONE: The World Cup.

I've never really told anyone, but I would trade all my Champions League medals and all my FISA 'Best Player in The World' trophies for The World Cup.

After all, it's the one trophy that has cemented the likes of Marantini and Lelé as the best players in the world.

I've been so close to winning it, and the truth is, that at 35 years old now, I know this would be my last chance to win it.

Go to page 106

CHAPTER 11

THINGS WENT FROM STRENGTH TO STRENGTH AFTER MY first FISA 'Best Player in The World' award. I had become Catalonia's top scorer and even won a couple more championships and Champions Leagues.

That's why I felt so confident going into this World Cup in Brazil. We had a great team, and well, to be honest, it had never felt like playing soccer came so easily to me. I had won nearly every game I had played in in the last three years!

⚽ ⚽ ⚽

The hairs on the back of my neck tingled as I roared my country's national anthem before the semi-final against The Netherlands at the World Cup.

The all-too-familiar orange jerseys lined up opposite us as we began the customary pre-game handshakes. The opposing captain, Dick Van Virg shook everyone's hand apart from mine. Instead, he gave me a pat on the shoulder, covered his mouth from prying TV cameras, and whispered in my ear:

"I don't shake hands with cheats," before running off to the center circle, knees up high, in an attempt to warm up his legs.

I felt anger boil up within me, and was very close to chasing after him before my teammate grabbed me tightly by the arm.

"They are doing it on purpose. They *want* you to react this way. Just let your *soccer* do the talking."

He was right, I caught a glance of the opposing manager and he was winking at Van Virg, as if to say: 'keep winding him up, he'll crumble eventually.'

The game was evenly poised at 2-2 after 120 minutes of soccer. Everyone was playing for penalties at this stage. It was obvious given that half the players on the field were cramping up.

Out of nowhere, I found myself chasing a 30 yard clearance that had me up against the Dutch keeper to decide who would go to the final. It was a simple one-on-one with the keeper, and I *never* missed these. He made himself big but left the bottom right hand side of his goal exposed.

I opened up my body, took a step forward to take the shot and… WALLOP!

"REFEREE! HE'S DIVING! BOOK HIM FOR DIVING!"

Van Virg had just clattered me from behind and kicked away my supporting leg as I was ready to take the shot. What he was saying to the referee was clearly an attempt to deflect the attention away from what he had done.

The referee showed him a straight red card, but not before Van Virg spat at the ball as I put in on the penalty spot.

"I told you you were a cheater. I barely touched

you. Karma will come back to haunt you as you take this kick - just wait and see..." His words lingering as he walked off the field.

I stood there waiting for the whistle. I had one kick to take to send my team through to the final of the World Cup.

Time stood still.

It seemed like hours as the referee cleared the 18-yard box from opposing defenders trying to stand in front of my teammates.

"Just hit it hard and down the middle. Hard and down the middle. Hard. Middle. Low. Hard. Middle. Low." I kept repeating inside my head.

This was not the time to try anything silly.

PEEEEEEEEEEP.

The referee blew his whistle and I ran six yards towards the ball.

I knew exactly what I wanted to do, and without an extra thought in my head, I hammered that ball as hard as I could. It was hard. It was down the middle. But it wasn't low.

I saw the ball rising to the skies...

"Oh no," I thought. "Had I hit it too high?!"

I was frozen to the spot with anxiety for a fraction of a second before I saw the ball hit the roof of the net.

The stadium erupted. 50,000 adoring fans cheered as I got clambered on by teammates.

A 123rd minute winning penalty that sent us through to the World Cup final. Surely it was our time to bring the most coveted trophy in the world back home!

"What has even happened in the last 110 minutes?!" I found myself asking as I looked up to the stadium clock at the Marbaná Stadium in Rio de Janeiro. It was the final of the World Cup and I was so focused on winning this game that the game itself had passed me by.

It all seemed a bit of a blur. I had to wake up from this slumber. It felt as if the enormity of the occasion had got to me. Sure, I had created a few good chances, but I was running on autopilot.

10 minutes to go before we go to penalties. And we had some confident penalty takers in our squad. It's in the bag. I'm 10 minutes from potentially achieving my lifelong dream and becoming a World Cup winner!

"C'mon boys! More of the same! Just 10 minutes to go," I shouted back at my teammates as the Germans zig-zagged the ball around our midfielders.

The ball was looped to the edge of our box, where Morris Gatze, the young emerging German striker, brought it down with one deft touch of his left thigh.

He immediately unleashed a rocket with his right foot that nestled into the top right-hand corner of our goal.

German players shoved my back as they rushed to congratulate Gatze. 110 minutes of holding out, and my dream vanished with this one freak shot.

We tried in the last 10 minutes to get something back, but the Germans simply took the ball to the corner flag.

The referee blew his whistle and I collapsed to the ground.

This was everything I wanted. Everything I had *ever* wanted. I would trade anything for this one trophy. *How could it have been taken so cruelly away?* I thought, as I collapsed into a crying mess in the center circle.

The rest of the evening was a hazy mess. I had to pretend to be happy as I was named the best player of the tournament, but I really didn't care about that. I just wanted my hands on the World Cup. Nothing else mattered.

⚽ ⚽ ⚽

"Don't *hit it hard and down the middle. NOT hard and not down the middle."*

Only two years had passed since our World Cup loss to Germany, and we again found ourselves in the spiritual home of soccer, The Marbaná Stadium.

It was testament to the strength in character of the lads in our team that only two years after losing a major final, we *again* found ourselves in a major final.

Sure, it wasn't the World Cup, but the Continental Championships is the second best international tournament, and I desperately wanted to win something for the people of my country.

As a country, we hadn't won anything in close to 20 years, and I knew how important this was to the happiness of my people back home. Especially given the terrible economic situation the country had just been through.

The game had finished 0-0, these finals are always a nervy affair where neither team wants to lose, and it had come down to penalties. The good old lottery that penalties inevitably seem to always be!

I was first to take the penalty.

"Don't hit it hard and down the middle. Not hard and not down the middle."

My last three penalties were hard and down the middle, so I knew the keeper would be expecting that.

As I lined up to take the shot I opened my body up to pretend I was going left. I was always meaning to deceive the keeper and go right for this penalty, but out of nowhere, a last minute decision came over me to 'double bluff' the keeper, so I ended up kicking it left, and at a comfortable height for the keeper.

He guessed the direction of the ball. I had made the height too easy for him and he effortlessly punched the ball away. *"For Goodness sake!"* I thought, sadness and shame descending upon me.

I've left my teammates with a tall mountain to climb.

What happened next was a bit of a blur. I couldn't stop thinking of how I'd let down millions of people back in my home country.

The opposing team converted all their penalties and we lost 4-5 on the night. All because of *my* mistake and indecisiveness. I should have stuck to my plan and kicked right.

My teammates gathered round me in one big group hug as the opposition celebrated winning the Continental Championship.

"You single handedly took us here," "There's *nothing you could have done, brother," "Chin up, skipper,"* were some of the words being said to me. I was devastated. Inconsolable. All because I had been indecisive about taking my penalty.

That indecisiveness kept me awake every night for three weeks. I lived through that recurring nightmare in my dreams every night. I had wasted *the biggest* opportunity of my life to win our country one of the greatest trophies available. An opportunity, which at my age, would probably *never* come again.

⚽ ⚽ ⚽

My phone vibrated as I saw my mom's WhatsApp message come through:

> Probably best to stay away from social media today, honey.

The phone buzzed immediately after with another message from my mom:

> And don't watch the news or buy any newspapers. We love you and we're here for you. xox

There's nothing like someone telling you *not* to do something to encourage you to do it.

I opened up my social apps and saw that my name was trending. I had expected that in all fairness - I had just cost my national team the chance to win the continental trophy. What I didn't expect was the level of hate I was getting from the press and my fellow countrymen and women.

"Go play for Spain - you've been in Catalonia long enough for us to know that you feel more Spanish than from our own country!" Spewed our best-known TV Reporter, Pies Worgan.

I mean, the guy *was* an idiot, but what hurt most was reading the comments under his video.

100% Agree.

I couldn't have put it better.

Never really liked Pies Worgan, but he's talking some sense here.

These sorts of comments were getting hundreds of thousands of likes.

The most liked photo in the thread was a picture someone took outside The Hilton Hotel in the city center. Someone had created a life-sized dummy of me for people to throw tomatoes at!

That last picture was hard to take. I shut my laptop screen straight away and pulled the bed cover over my head. I was hoping to hide the tears. I don't know who I was trying to hide them from. I was all alone. I *felt* all alone.

⚽ ⚽ ⚽

It had been three weeks since we got eliminated from the Continental Championship and things with the press hadn't got any easier.

That dummy of me was no longer there, but it was only because it had been burned in front of a crowd of 300 people chanting *"Go back to Spain! Go back to Spain!"*

My phone rang. It was Mom.

"How are you feeling, honey?" she said.

"I'm okay, Mom. You'll be glad to know that I've made my decision."

"That's great to hear, darling. What time is the press conference?"

"It's in 10 minutes. I've got to go as the Press Officer is calling me. Love you!"

As I walked into the press conference, the sound of clicking cameras deafened me. Who knew so many clicks could make such a racket?! And the flashes! It really is an attack on all my senses. I couldn't get my head straight.

As I sat down next to the national team's Press Officer, a sea of microphones lay in front of me.

As she begins to talk, the flashes and camera clicks subside. I can finally start to make sense of what's going on and catch her last few words…

"...and that's why he's called this press conference. To make this very special announcement."

She turns her head to me and gives me a gentle nod. It was my time to speak.

As I clear my throat, a million cameras click in unison.

"Thank you all. I wanted to let everyone know that…"

DECISION TIME

If you want to let everyone know that you're retiring from international soccer because you've had enough of the abuse given by the press and the fans, go to page 54

If you want to let everyone know that it's time to stop the hate and negativity and focus on getting ready for the Continental Championship and the World Cup in the United Arab Emirates in two years' time, go to page 29

CHAPTER 12

MONCHEN KICK-OFF. THERE'S ONE MINUTE LEFT ON THE clock.

Through exhaustion or fear, they lose the ball quickly, and it spills to my feet. I knock it past a midfielder and wrap my foot around it, toward Oli down the left wing. He heads goal-wards, twisting and faking, trying to find space to shoot. He wins a corner.

Beckenham runs to the corner spot, aware of the ever-counting clock. It's now or never.

He curls it across the face of the goal, the Monchen players frozen to the spot. I gamble at the front post and glance a header to my right. The ball bounces unclaimed in-front of the German goal-keeper, rising from the ground as our super-sub Oli flicks a foot at it – sending it flying hard into the roof of the net! NO WAY! He's done it!

With only 10 seconds left of the game we make it 2-1. WE HAVE DONE IT. The Treble is finally ours!

I sprint past German defenders who are punching the grass in agony and frustration and make my way to Oli who's sliding on his knees celebrating the most dramatic goal the Champions League has ever seen!

I have never known such pandemonium. It felt like the whole of Manchester were there in the stadium, such was the volume of the cheer and force of joy.

It is the happiest I have ever seen Sir Alec. His fists raised in a historic win. The pink face of victory. "Soccer. Bloody Hell!" he says to reporters. I had never seen him lost for words.

Yet there we were. The first team ever to win a treble. Wow.

⚽⚽⚽

That summer there was a lot of interest for me from all the biggest clubs across Europe. I was happy at Manchester, a domestic *and* European Champion... However, I did still have a slight, nagging desire to go to Spain.

I was at the training ground on the first day of pre-season, being put through my paces by the coaches. As I fell to the ground in a fit of sweat and tiredness, I heard Sir Alec call my name.

"Son, ya got a minute. Need to talk." I knew he was serious.

I followed him inside. "You've been a star playa' fa' us for years now." I smiled; you take compliments whenever you can from a man like Sir Alec.

"But I kno' ya family and I kno' ya' background." He did, my mom loved him. "We've had a serious offer fram' Catalonia for ya' an' I kno' ya'd want tae kno' that."

Something stirred in my stomach. A mix of excitement and guilt.

"'Serious', as in you're considering it, boss?" I asked.

"Aye, serious enough tha' I'm tellin' ya' now." He was basically telling me it was my decision. Go to FC Catalonia, having won everything but leaving my friends and soccer family behind or stay, keep winning for Manchester, comfortable with an incredible soccer career.

"I'll have to think about it, boss. That's a BIG decision." He patted me on the shoulder, his way of showing respect, and nodded. "Don' think for too long tho' aye son."

DECISION TIME

If you thank Sir Alec but make the move to FC Catalonia, go to page 136

If you thank Sir Alec and stay at Manchester in the hope of becoming a legend for the Devils, go to page 163

CHAPTER 13

WITH INTEREST FROM FC CATALONIA STILL RUNNING through my head, I looked in the mirror, the cut was bad, but it wasn't *that* bad. "If I want this to really blow up, I'm going to have to make this stand out." I scraped back my long hair and fixed it in place with a headband, making sure everyone would be able to see the cut and the oversized cross stitch plaster I had slapped on. The phone rang again, it was my agent. "I've tipped off the press, work your magic."

Sure enough, as I arrived at the training ground, the entrance was packed with the global press, hungry for an exclusive on the fallout. I wound down my window and gave them a sorrowful look, making sure they could all see the cut on my forehead. The story was already written for them - I'd been attacked by my own manager, but was still showing up at training like a true professional.

Still in the car and leaving the media circus behind me, I hadn't even reached the parking lot when my phone rang again, this time it was the chairman. "You won't be needed in training today. We've accepted a bid from FC Catalonia. Your career here is over."

Go to page 136

CHAPTER 14

THEY SAY THAT IF YOU DO ANYTHING FOR 10,000 HOURS you'll become an expert in it. I had been taking free kicks since I was a kid. I was ready for this moment.

I could hear the shouts for a cross at the back post, but I was phasing those out. I knew what to do and where to put the ball.

I took three steps back. Looking at the goal, I analyzed the position of the goalkeeper and the Chilean wall positioned in front of me.

I took a deep breath, readied myself and ran to the ball. I was almost side-on to it, giving my foot the best chance of wrapping around the ball, curling it away from the goalkeeper.

PUFFT! A clean hit off my left foot. It felt right.

I watched it sail over the wall, spinning away from the keeper and into the top left of the goal.

BOOM! The stadium exploded in a roar of passion and happiness. I ran to the fans, my arms aloft, shouting as loud as I have ever shouted.

I jumped, landing on two feet, fist clenched, standing in front of the crowd sharing their joy.

We had done it. We had qualified for the World Cup. My last chance at international success.

BRING IT ON.

Go to page 106

CHAPTER 15

There was a lot of noise in the media about me moving and how, if I wanted to be one of the game's greats, I needed to move to one of the marquee teams in Europe. However, I didn't necessarily agree with that. I loved being at Westfalen, and although I could have earned more money elsewhere, I felt a sense of duty to try and bring success to the club both domestically and in European competition.

Over the next few years, I became the star player in my national team and broke all goalscoring records at club level and at international level. We won more league and cup titles at Westfalen, and I extended my contract there, playing on until retirement.

Internationally, I led my country to two World Cup finals but came away as runners-up both times. I smashed the goalscoring record with 103 international goals but, sadly, won no international trophies.

At Westfalen, we continued to exchange league and cup titles with Bayer Monchen regularly, never finishing outside the top four. We reached two more European Cup finals but could never quite bring the silverware home.

I broke all club records at Westfalen, playing a record 600 games, becoming the club's all-time leading goalscorer with 289 goals, and winning seven league titles and six domestic cups. When I finally retired, the club honored me with a statue outside the stadium. Watching them unveil the statue with my young family, my parents and my sister beside me, was truly one of the proudest days of my life.

⚽ ⚽ ⚽

I sometimes allowed myself to wonder what would have happened if I had gone to another club, but I was happy to have achieved so much in my career at a great club surrounded by great people.

AND JUST LIKE THAT MY SOCCER CAREER ENDED.

CHAPTER 16

I SEND THE BALL STRAIGHT BACK INTO THE PATH OF Daveed, who lets it run across his body before smashing it into the top corner with his iconic pink cleats.

He jogs off cooly to the crowd as we jump into the stands to celebrate with the fans.

The referee blows for full-time. We won 2-1 and I helped bring a long overdue trophy to the mighty London Lilywhites!

As we're walking up to collect our trophies, Daveed hands me his cleats, "You earned this today l'enfant. Goal *and* an assist." He patted me on the shoulder. "Swoosh will be calling you tomorrow."

Go to page 5

CHAPTER 17

"I WANTED TO LET EVERYONE KNOW THAT THE LAST three weeks have been very tough for me and my family."

I was focused on staring at one bright light on top of a camera at the end of the room as I continued.

"No one should be subjected to the level of abuse and hatred that I've been the victim of over the last few days, not least a soccer player who has given everything he's got for his country."

The camera clicks were incessant - drowning out every word I said.

"That is why, it is with a heavy heart, that I announce my retirement from soccer with immediate effect".

There was a collective gasp from the assembled press in the room, before an even bigger flurry of camera clicks began flashing away.

"The behavior shown towards me by fans has been nothing short of abhorrent. It has made me fall out of love with a game I so dearly cherished.

I have also spoken to my club, who have agreed to terminate my contract by mutual consent.

I'd like to thank you all for your support throughout the years. If you could please now respect mine and my family's privacy, that would very much be appreciated. Thank you."

I stood up from my chair to an avalanche of questions from reporters. I couldn't make out a single one of their questions. Not because they were all talking over each other, but because I caught a glance of my wife and kids waiting for me through a side door.

I was ready to go home with them for good. That made me happy.

Whilst ignoring all the flashes and flurry of questions, I made a beeline for my family and my new life.

AND JUST LIKE THAT MY SOCCER CAREER ENDED.

CHAPTER 18

It's been a whirlwind, signing terms, saying goodbye to my family and friends and finally arriving for my medical in Germany. All those hours of extra training and hard work meant I flew through my medical and was joining up with the first team well in time for pre-season training.

It was going to be difficult adjusting to a new country, and being away from family and on my own for the first time was definitely daunting. My parents had arranged everything with the club and to start with I'd be sharing a house with some of the other young players who had recently signed, including a young midfielder and fellow countryman called Esteban Sanchez who'd recently signed from FC Riveria. We'd be studying German together and had a staff member assigned to us for our wellbeing. The club was really going out of its way to look after me and this was such a big opportunity, however, I couldn't help but feel a little sad when I thought of home and how much I would miss my old life, my friends, my family...home. At least in Esteban I would have someone around who spoke the same language as me.

I was in awe. Some of the biggest names in Europe, in world soccer in fact, were at the club. This little country town boy was now playing in one of the biggest leagues in the world and mixing with some of the biggest players in the game!

Despite feeling the enormity of it all, I knew I hadn't made it yet, just getting into the team would be a huge task. It would require dedication, hard work and taking my chances when they did come my way.

In front of me in the team's pecking order was the club's best player: Ratan Zhivec. The imperious Swedish international and the team's main goal threat. His contract was up at the end of the season and the rumors were that he'd already agreed a deal behind the scenes to join Milano.

If I played well and was patient, perhaps I could be taking Zhivec's place in the team next year. In fact, my agent had been told as much when we were negotiating the contract, I was being signed as Zhivec's long-term replacement. He'd averaged a goal every one and half games in the last three seasons. I had big shoes to fill - the gigantic Swede standing at 6″4.

Go to page 70

CHAPTER 19

I LAUGHED AT MY AGENT. HE KNEW MY UPBRINGING; he'd met my mom. He knew the answer.

"Let's go in, shall we? I can't wait to get that number 10 on my back."

My agent smiled and put his arm around my shoulder. I was waiting for him to ruffle my hair, but he didn't. Maybe I was becoming less of a kid in his eyes. FINALLY.

I followed the grinning chairwoman and my smiling agent through her house into her garden. I say garden, it was more of a forest that stretched on for as far as the eye could see.

"Right, let's get this deal sorted, shall we?" She said, already handing me a pen and showing me the contract on the table.

"I've read it, we're good to go. It's everything you want." Said my agent. "Even the goal bonus." He added with a wink. Wow, I was about to do this.

I took the pen and thought about my family, where I'd come from and how proud they would be of me. I wished they could have been here to see this.

As I signed my name on the paper, the chairwoman jumped up and cheered my name. She then ran onto her lawn, still wearing her high-heels and smashed a soccer into the top corner of the goal. Impressive.

"Can we take a photo?" I asked my agent and the excited chairwoman, who was still celebrating her goal on the lawn. "I want to remember this moment."

"For YOU..." cried the chairwoman. "This club will do anything."

Go to page 24

CHAPTER 20

I CAN'T BELIEVE I'D BEEN SO WORRIED ABOUT GOING out, I'm having a blast! I'm closer to my teammates now than I ever have been, and those drinks they offer me, well they taste disgusting but it makes me feel like I fit in when I drink them with the boys.

It's the fourth night in a row we've been out, partying, dancing, staying up late and even chatting to girls. We've got a cup game tomorrow against a team we beat 5-0 earlier in the season, so we shouldn't have anything to worry about, this is the life!

⚽ ⚽ ⚽

I look around at my teammates, hands on hips; '*how are we 1-0 down to this team*?' It has not been a good game for any of us, we're losing with only minutes left on the clock. Lose this and we are out of the cup, that doesn't happen to us - we *just* don't lose!

I spot Gus on the wing breaking into space so I

make a slightly delayed run off the defender to the back post as I call for the ball. Sure enough Gus sees me and pings a ball in, clearing the first defender, then narrowly past the second defender. It's slightly behind me so I adjust my position swiftly and expertly to hit the ball on a sideways scissor-kick. I leap, time pauses for a moment and I swing my foot at it.

Peeep, Peeep, Peeep!

As the final whistle blows, I look up and see the opposition players running to each other in celebration...I had completely mistimed my scissor kick. Instead I ended up as an awkward twisted lump on the floor, and the ball had sailed out for a goal kick.

As I trudge off the field, head down, my manager comes over to me and points out a figure on the sidelines talking to the opposition team's striker.

He's dressed in club gear from FC Catalonia, one of the world's leading team's. It's a club I've dreamed of playing for for as long as I can remember. "You see that man over there, he's a scout from FC Catalonia, you've blown any chance you had of making it in Spain with that performance!"

AND JUST LIKE THAT MY SOCCER CAREER ENDED.

CHAPTER 21

We won the Cup fairly comfortably against Oldcastle United, one of the country's most heavily supported teams. Teddingham and Skols doing the damage on the day to bring Manchester Devils their second trophy of the season, just one more trophy left now to complete a historic TREBLE! Sir Alec allowed us a few hours at the famous Werberly Stadium to celebrate before taking the trophy from our captain, Beano, and stating very firmly: "You still owe me the big one."

Next weekend we were playing the famous German side Bayer Monchen in the Champions League final at FC Catalonia's incredible Campo Nuevo stadium in Spain.

We had played against Bayer Monchen twice already this season, drawing in both games during the group stages. They were tough, smart and ruthless. This was going to be the hardest test of my entire career.

I couldn't wait.

I was sitting in my chair in the locker room with my soccer jersey hanging proudly above me. Beano and Skolsy were in suits. They were both suspended for this match, so had to miss out. Having to play against this Monchen side with them was hard enough, but without them? It was going to take some kind of miracle.

Beano sat next to me. "How are you feeling?" He nudged his elbow into my arm, snapping me from the daydream I was lost in. "I know these games can be intimidating and I know you're gutted that me and Skols can't join you in the middle, but know we're there in spirit and fighting with you from the sideline in every tackle you go in for."

I nodded, as he gave me a firm handshake. He got up to leave and then added; "Besides, if any of them give you a kick, I'll be waiting in the tunnel at half-time. Let them know that, yeah?"

The locker room erupted into laughter. Beano always knew what to say.

Sir Alec cleared his throat and quickly earned the silence of the room. He ushered Beano and Skolsy to his side and gestured toward them. "We win, draw and lose as a team. These two are the best in the world in their positions and have earned the right to play in this game." He smiled at the pair of them. "Unfortunately it wasn't to be for them, but that's soccer for ya – it can be a cruel mistress."

He slowly scanned the players sitting around the edges of the locker room, catching each individual by the eye. "Right now, you have the chance to do what is mostly unthinkable for the majority of soccer clubs.

No club has ever won the treble. It is time to write this club, and your names, into the soccer history books."

With that he turned around and walked out. Beano walked up to our Danish goalkeeper and handed him his captain's armband. "I've not washed this all season and look where we are."

Peter lifted his arm, his gloves already fixed to his hands so unable to put the band on himself. "Peter is your captain today and by God will he let you know it!"

Everyone cheered as the keeper raised a thumb to respond. Beano then swiveled to me, "…but this lad here is your leader on the field." I gulped.

"This guy has shown guts and glory in every game this season. Despite his age, he fights with experience, confidence and skill," Beano beamed. "Give this lad the ball and we've got a chance against the Germans."

We all stood up, pulled on our jerseys and marched in single file through the door to the tunnel. There was nothing else to say. Just 90 minutes to decide our fate and destiny.

⚽ ⚽ ⚽

Disaster within six minutes.

Our defender Bobby Rohnson made a clumsy challenge on Monchen's big striker Kasron Tancker on the edge of our box. I lined up in the wall with Beckenham, Teddingham and Jesker, one of our Swedish players who had joined me in the middle in Skolsy's absence. We all agreed to jump to block the ball but the German free kick taker cleverly placed a low shot around us and into the corner of our goal. Our captain Smike was flat-footed and caught out. We were now 1-0 down and with an angry captain. Not a great mix.

Game very much on.

It took some time, but we gained control of the game. Our back four were comfortable and kept the 6′4″ Tancker in their back pockets…just.

Riggsy, our skillful winger, was playing out of position but causing the Monchen defense all sorts of problems. Andy up top was running his red socks off, creating space for our midfield and tiring their center backs, but without the passing of Skolsy available to us, we just couldn't find a break-through.

We went in behind at the break and fully prepared for an infamous Sir Alec verbal barrage.

I put my arm around Rohnson as we trudged to the locker room. "Head up mate, we've all made mistakes this half. You were great afterwards." He nodded, his fear halved. For now.

Sir Alec was waiting for us. Stood in the middle of the room, his hands on his hips and his face a similar shade to beetroot. "WHAT THE HELL WAZ THA'?!" He screamed, knocking the tactics board over onto the floor.

He pointed at Rohnson. "You lad. We don' make tackles like tha' there…AND SIX MINUTES IN."

He turned and pointed at Peter. "You stood still like bloody Mickel-an-gelos David. If you wan' ta' pretend to be a statue, I'll send ya' to a' museum. Ya old enough!"

Sir Alec stopped for a second, until he found me. "Big game playas' turn up in tha' big games. Where are' ya' lad? Are ya' fit ta' wear this wee jersey?" I kept his eye-line.

"You got somethin' ta' say laddy?"

DECISION TIME

If you calmly defend your teammates, go to page 81

If you get into an argument with Sir Alec, go to page 145

CHAPTER 22

"Get off me," I scream, accidentally knocking my teammate and friend off his feet and onto the ground. I ran at the referee like a red flag to a bull; I had had enough of him today.

"Are you cheating ref? Have you been paid by the Brazilians?!" A stupid accusation but it was too late. I had let anger win and there was no controlling it now.

The referee looked shocked and immediately changed the card in his hand from yellow to red. "Get off my field right now. You have dived all game, and tried to cheat the Brazilians out of the ball by incessantly throwing yourself on the floor." He was shouting back at me now, "…and I had heard you were extraordinary, so much for that." He turned to walk away from me.

As if lifting out of my body, I watched in horror from above as I charged the referee and pushed him hard on the chest. He stumbled backwards and landed awkwardly on his back. The stadium went quiet. A long, eerie silence. I had made a huge mistake.

Before the Brazilian players could get to me, one of my defenders grabbed me by my collar, pushing me towards the tunnel. "Get off this field. What the hell are you thinking?!" He looked me right in the eyes. "We needed you and you do something *this* stupid? JUST GO."

I trudged past the technical area, past my players and the manager. He stared at me with cold blank disappointment. "I would never have thought you would do this to your country on such a big international stage." He turned away.

That was it. That was the last time I would be selected for my national team. Such promise ahead of me, quickly popped like a pin on a balloon.

I wandered down the tunnel in tears, unsure what was left of my soccer career.

⚽ ⚽ ⚽

It took 24 hours for FC Catalonia to cancel my contract. FISA had banned me from soccer for two years with immediate effect, leaving my club no choice but to part ways. I'd gone from an international soccer star at Spain's biggest club to a soccer player with no club or country.

⚽ ⚽ ⚽

After a very difficult 18 months back home with my family and without having stepped foot on a field, I was offered a chance to train in Turkey at Sikbektas.

However, in the dry Turkish heat, on my first session with their physio, I turned sharply and felt a sharp excruciating pain in my knee. OUCH. I couldn't stand or put any weight on my leg and was once again reduced to tears. The reaction of the Turkish physio team didn't look positive as they carried me by stretcher to the medical room.

A quick scan proved I had just injured the anterior cruciate ligament in my knee. Two years recovery time.

I called the only person I could in this situation... "I think I'm done Mom. I can't play for another 18 months, and I can't even legally kick a ball professionally for six months." I pulled back the tears. "I think it's time to give up."

AND JUST LIKE THAT MY SOCCER CAREER ENDED.

CHAPTER 23

I ARRIVED AT TRAINING EARLY, EAGER TO MAKE A GOOD impression. I persuaded my compatriot Sanchez to come in early with me as well, mainly so I wasn't completely alone on my first day.

Guided by the receptionist, we made our way through the grand foyer and down a long corridor displaying portraits of some of Westfalen's past heroes. We then reached the training ground locker rooms.

I took a deep breath, calming any nerves, then pushed the door open. Deep in conversation were two players who I instantly recognized as Ratan Zhivec and German international and club captain Maro Ruiz. Neither of them so much as glanced at us as we took our seats and started getting changed into our new Westfalen training uniform.

I looked around and chose an empty space to sit in, and Sanchez did the same. As soon as my backside hit the seat, I heard Zhivec, without even looking up, loudly proclaim: "You can't sit there, that seat is for first team players only." Not wanting to cause a problem, I moved and chose another seat on the far side of the locker room. However, as soon as I sat, I again heard the same words in the same voice, "you can't sit there, that seat is for first team players only." This happened another three times before I realized Zhivec and Ruiz were laughing; they were making fun of us.

I felt myself getting angry. I hated bullies. I needed to say something immediately or they would walk all over us for the rest of the season, but if I did say something and annoy the captain and the star player then what; perhaps I'd never get into the first team at all...

DECISION TIME

To confront Zhivec & Ruiz, go to page 174

To say nothing and bide your time, go to page 74

CHAPTER 24

The Gunnerbury full back was closing on me and I was running out of time to float the ball in accurately. Time for Plan B…get the ball near the penalty spot and hope that Renato Conaldo is first to it.

I wrapped my foot around the ball and curled it at pace toward the middle of Gunnerbury's penalty box. It was out of my hands, time for fate *and* that soccer genius's big brain to get it in their goal.

I watched in slow-motion as he changed his body position, turned his back to goal and angled his legs to pull off something truly audacious. He was going to try an overhead kick.

The Gunnerbury defenders and goalkeeper were frozen in position. There was nothing they could do to stop him other than hope he misread the flight of the ball and landed in a heap on the grass.

Conaldo never misreads it though. As the ball reached his body, he spun, arched his back, and jumped to bicycle kick the ball in mid-air back toward the Gunnerbury goal. It hit the top corner like a rocket.

YES! 2-2. We were back in the game.

I turned and caught a look at Sir Alec. I was hoping I'd changed his half-time plans of screaming at me in-front of the whole team and coaching squad. He saw me and raised a thumb. Phew.

The whistle blew. Half-Time. There was everything still to play for.

Go to page 127

CHAPTER 25

I DECIDED TO BIDE MY TIME AND LET MY SOCCER DO THE talking. After all, that's what had always worked for me in the past. The locker room began to fill up with other players, and I decided to say nothing. I chose another seat, fully expecting to be told to move again by Zhivec, but I was saved by the manager walking in with the coaches and telling everyone to get out onto the training field. I pulled my socks on, showing no emotion. The truth was that I was hurting inside. I felt embarrassed and angry. I knew that the only way I would win anyone's respect and my place in the team would be through what I could do on the field, not what I said off it. As I got up to head out, Zhivec walked past, towering above me. He looked at me and gave me a sly smile as if to say, "Watch out, or I'll eat you for breakfast and spit you out."

⚽⚽⚽

Training was a typical pre-season session with lots of running and fitness drills. It was intense, and I felt the burn, but I was doing okay and knew I could push harder if I needed to. The fitness drills ended with a beep test, where your fitness was tested with short sprints between two cones, and if you didn't reach the cone as the time intervals decreased, you were disqualified. It was a drill I used to practice at home with my dad, and I knew I was good at it. As players dropped out, I found myself in the final four with Zhivec, Sanchez, and Ruiz. I had plenty of energy left and knew I could probably go on and win it, but after the incident earlier, I was keen not to draw too much attention to myself or show up the established players, Zhivec and Ruiz, so I slowed down and dropped out. Zhivec, who had been first placed in this drill every year since he joined, went on to win again.

The training session ended with a small-sided game. Ruiz and Zhivec were on the opposing team, and although I knew I could run rings around some of them, I made sure not to do anything too flashy and concentrated on passing and moving the ball. I made sure no one could get near me but also didn't show off too much.

The rest of the session went without many incidents, and I made a good, if not amazing, account of myself. I did nothing wrong, but I also played within myself, not wanting to draw unwanted attention or embarrass any of the established players. As we headed back to the locker rooms, I hung back a little and walked with Sanchez. He put his arm around me. "So, what was that all about?" he asked. I pretended that I didn't know what he was talking about. "I don't understand you. You could have won that beep test easily, and I know you could beat most of those guys with your dribbling if you wanted to. Why are you holding back?" I went to answer him, but the coach interrupted and asked for a word with me. I gave Sanchez a smile and a nod, and he jogged off, leaving me and the coach alone.

"I heard you two talking, and I noticed it myself. Look, you don't need to worry about guys like Zhivec or any of them. We brought you to Westfalen because we know what you can do on the field. So, I want to see that from you. I can tell you're a nice, polite boy, and trust me, you'll win the established players round pretty quickly if you show them what you can do. If you don't want to do it on the training field yet, then I want you to do it on the actual field against proper opposition. I'll give you some first team minutes in the coming games. Make sure you show everyone what you can do out there!"

Go to page 83

CHAPTER 26

In the last week during training we had been practicing half volleys. Honing our skills in being able to hit the ball at pace just as it lands and bounces back off the turf. And now was as good a time as ever to implement what we'd been practicing for the last few days. I stepped to the ball and flicked it up off the ground quickly, giving it a shallow bounce, before running my laces through it like a steam-train.

It flew goal-bound. The Lilywhites defense could only watch as the ball sailed over their heads and directly at the top right corner of the goal. It was moments like these when everything moved in slo-mo. Their goalkeeper desperately scrambled across the goal line as the ball rifled off the post and into the empty net. My teammates rushed to me to celebrate. The fans jumped out of the red seats to embrace their loved ones around them.

I was already off toward the supporters. Jumping into the celebrating fans. WOW.

WE WERE AHEAD. 2-1. The league was ours again!

I quickly glanced over to Sir Alec on the touchline. He raised a thumb and then mouthed, "TOLD YOU." He had a point.

One trophy down, TWO TO GO.

Go to page 62

CHAPTER 27

"WHO ARE YOU AGAIN, MATE?" SAID THE SECURITY guard at Werberly as I explained that I had lost the bracelet that gets me into the VIP section of the stadium.

"I play for Al Qaffa. C'mon, man!" I start to get heated.

"It was only six years ago that I scored the winning goal here to win FC Catalonia the Champions League! You *must* remember me?!" I plead.

"I'm afraid I can't let you in without a VIP bracelet, sir," was the monotone response from the burly guard.

Dejected, I trod down the steps of Werberly. Ever since I had taken that £300 million contract in Saudi Arabia things had gone terribly wrong for me.

I had a target on my back as soon as I joined the league and suffered a horrible leg break in my fourth game.

It took me a year to recover, and when I came back... well, it just wasn't the same. Maybe it was the lack of competitive edge in their league, I just didn't find the motivation to perform after that.

This guest appearance at Werberly was my last official duty with the club as they weren't renewing my contract.

But not even that, a token role in a Champions League final game, went my way.

I was well and truly forgotten. I cast a forlorn figure as I walked down Werberly Lane whilst the Champions League final was still being played in the stadium behind me.

I was nothing but a washed up has-been.

AND JUST LIKE THAT MY SOCCER CAREER ENDED.

CHAPTER 28

I LOOKED AROUND THE ROOM, SOME OF MY TEAMMATES catching my eye as I was about to do the unthinkable.

"Yeah, I do actually, Sir Alec." I said as Sir Alec lifted himself higher, puffing out his chest, ready for confrontation.

"It's true we started slowly and we maybe let the stage get to us mentally." I looked at young Rohnson and smiled. "But we have shown strength and resilience to grab control of the game since."

Sir Alec held my eye contact, but his purple glow was fading.

"Peter has made some fantastic saves since the goal and led us from the back." The captain stood up and smiled my way in support. "Rohnson made a mistake but has been incredible since."

The door opened behind us, as Beano and Skolsy quietly entered the room.

"Andy and Wight have run the Monchen defense ragged and a goal is coming. Riggsy came really close with a header just before half-time." My confidence growing as nobody interrupted.

"All we need to do is more of the same." I realized I had the room's attention. "Keep up the energy, keep up the pressure and keep up the battle in the midfield. We've got them on the ropes."

The players cheered and I saw Beano clap slowly in support.

Sir Alec cleared his throat. Silencing the room.

"FINALLY. A bit of wee' leadership from this magic lad in the middle." He walked up to me and patted me on the back – high praise from Sir Alec.

"Everyone get in close." The team joined in for a huddle. "If we bottle tha' desire 'n keep the belief, we will win thus' game and tha' treble. They will tire 'n we have some great lads coming off tha' bench to finish tha' game off." He nodded toward our benched strikers, Teddingham and Oli.

Suddenly, out of nowhere Beano let rip his loudest and deepest roar to date. It ripped through the tension in the room and lifted us an extra foot. We were ready.

Go to page 101

CHAPTER 29

I PICKED UP A SLIGHT INJURY IN TRAINING FROM A HARD tackle by one of the established players, which kept me out of the pre-season games. However, I was still able to work on my fitness, and the coach was sure to remind me of our conversation and his promise that I would get a chance to show what I can do in the first team once the season started. Life had been okay; I had made some good friends in Sanchez and some other teammates. Although there were a few incidents with Zhivec at the training ground, like him pushing in front of me in the canteen and hiding my training uniform, it was all school playground antics, and I tried not to let it get to me.

At Westfalen, we were expected to challenge for the league title and the Domestic Cup, and make a good account of ourselves in European competition. But realistically, we were the second biggest team in Germany, with Bayer Monchen being the favorites to win it all. Our opening game was against Josburg, who were expected to finish somewhere between the relegation places and mid-table. It was a game we should win.

With 83 minutes gone, we were 1-0 up with a goal in the first half from Zhivec. The coach called me over and told me to stretch; I was going on! The board went up with my number, and after a half-hearted handshake with the player I was replacing, Maro Ruiz, I sprinted across to get in position as the 80,000-seater stadium rose to its feet to applaud me.

I immediately latched onto a loose pass from a Josburg midfielder, and I was off, slaloming past one defender, then another, the ball glued to my feet. I approached the edge of the box and shifted my body weight, using my low center of gravity to send the defender one way as I moved outside of him and glided into the area. Another defender went to close me down as I cut inside and, seeing Zhivec unmarked on the edge of the area, I rolled the ball back to him. The pass was perfect and rolled across his body onto his stronger foot where he unleashed a rocket-powered strike. The crowd held their breath as it cannoned off the crossbar and was cleared away to safety by the Josburg defense. Zhivec jogged back past me, "Next time, Zhivec expects a better pass," and off we went. The clock ran down, and we won 1-0.

The next two games passed in similar circumstances; we won but not convincingly, and I managed to get a few minutes at the end of the games. I felt like I played well but didn't manage to get an assist or a goal.

Next up was a home game against Bayer Monchen, our biggest rivals for the title and the strongest and most prestigious team in Germany. I was boosted by the news that my family would be coming out for the game, all paid for by the club. Even better news however, was that the coach said that I would be starting the game!

⚽⚽⚽

With only five minutes of the game gone, I was played through by Ruiz, and as the Monchen goal-keeper came out expecting me to try and go around him, I deftly scooped the ball over him with the slightest of touches, dinking the ball up and into the net. I had just scored my first goal in Germany! I rushed over to the stands and pointed at my family who were celebrating wildly. The whole stadium was going crazy as I was mobbed by my teammates.

The game went by in a blur, everything happening so fast and frantically. I slowed my breathing down and concentrated on my skills. For me, everything went in slow-motion as I glided past players and put on the best performance of my life.

Just before half-time, I received a cutback pass from our winger and steered the ball into the top corner. Two goals in the first half, and against the best team in the country! The stadium felt like it was going to explode. *I* felt like I might explode!

The second half started in a similar manner, our defense containing the Monchen attack and spring-boarding us into great attacking positions. I was played through again, and with the keeper this time making the angle too tight, I spotted the onrushing Zhivec and squared the ball to him to make it 3-0.

The final whistle went, and we had won 3-0, with me scoring two and setting one up as well. What a way to introduce myself on my first home start! This was unbelievable; this was dreamland! 3-0 against our biggest rivals!

The coach liked what he saw, and as the season went on, I started most games, forming a deadly partnership with Zhivec on the field, if not so much off of it. By December, I had 15 goals and 10 assists, with Zhivec on 18 goals and three assists, none of which were for me.

⚽ ⚽ ⚽

After the winter break, it was announced that Zhivec would be leaving to sign for Milano at the end of the season. This news seemed to relax him and had a positive effect on the team. Although we would never be best friends, we became even more prolific on the field, with his goals and my goals and assists propelling us forward at the top of the league.

Going into the end of the season, all eyes were on our final fixture, which was away against our league rivals Bayer Monchen. We had done brilliantly this season and were level on points with them. The league title all came down to this one game!

⚽ ⚽ ⚽

All the hard work, all the ups and downs had come to this, a final game against our biggest rivals. The Monchen stadium was huge, historic, and intimidating, but having beaten them earlier in the season, we were confident we could beat them again and win the league title.

At half-time, the game was tied at 2-2. I had scored both, but Monchen's attacks had been relentless. They scored again to go 3-2 up in the 80th minute and sat back, trusting their defense to hold us out.

The tide turned and it was now all Westfalen, attack after attack being cleared by Monchen defenders. There were countless last-ditch tackles and big clearances as their defense got deeper and deeper, giving us less and less space to operate in going forward. As the clock ticked over into the 90th minute, I managed to lose my player outside on the left wing and sent an inch-perfect cross into Zhivec, who sent a thunderous header into the Monchen net. 3-3, but a point wasn't enough for us to win the league due to Monchen's superior goal difference.

There was no time to celebrate as we grabbed the ball and headed back to the center circle to get the game going as quickly as possible. The assistant referee held up his board, signaling there would be seven minutes of time added on. There were great cheers from our supporters; they sensed there was enough time for us to score, they believed we could do this!

With the game level at 3-3, the title looked to be heading to Monchen. As we headed into the 7th minute of time added on, I received the ball from a teammate and dribbled elegantly past two defenders, skipping through into the Monchen box. I was about to unleash the match-winning shot, when BAM! I was taken down from behind by a clumsy challenge. The ref pointed to the spot, awarding us a penalty!

Zhivec, who always took the penalties, snatched the ball up. He turned to me with his chest puffed out and stated emphatically, "Zhivec thinks the best player in the world should take this penalty kick." He nodded at me and then handed me the ball to take the penalty kick. "You have earned this, little smurf."

I had practiced this skill so many times in training, scored so many in matches back home, but nothing could compare to the feeling in this moment, the pressure, the expectation, the *nerves*...

I took a deep breath, and like I had always done, struck the ball perfectly with my instep, sending it rocketing past the hapless goalkeeper into the top corner.

With that, I completed my hat-trick and won the league title for Westfalen. I turned and ran celebrating; the noise was deafening as I was engulfed by my teammates. We had won the league title!

I was mobbed by my teammates, and had the crowd chanting my name from the stands, I finally felt accepted and at home in Germany. It was everything I had ever dreamed of! Even Zhivec and I were embracing as we held the German League trophy aloft in front of our adoring fans.

A few days later, I flew back home to be with my family for a couple of weeks. I was out shopping with my mom when the phone rang. It was my agent. My performances at Westfalen had been drawing attention from some of Europe's biggest clubs. He told me that Manchester Devils, one of the biggest clubs in world soccer, had been following my performances this season and were so impressed with my league-winning performance that they wanted to sign me.

. . .

DECISION TIME

To sign for Manchester Devils, go to page 153

To stay at Westfalen next season, go to page 92

CHAPTER 30

"WOAH, WOAH. WAIT." MY TEAMMATE HOLDS ME by my shoulders, trying to halt my red mist. "Take a breath, take a deep breath. Don't give him the chance to make your day worse."

Like hearing a distant voice in another room, I follow the words and take a long, deep breath in through my nose and count to 10. "That's it mate, we all know it's a penalty but he's not given it so suck it up and move on."

He now had his hand around my shoulders, steering me away from the referee. It was working, I felt better. Getting angry wasn't the answer, the team needed me on the field. I was no good to them if I was sent off.

The referee walked toward me, a smirk on his face, ready for me to lose it again. "You're lucky I didn't send you off just now. Any more dives and my red card becomes your best friend."

Taking one more deep breath, I nod to the referee and run back into position.

We went on to lose 3-0. I was gutted. We had let

the country down. As I was making that difficult walk back to the locker room after a defeat, I saw the manager marching over to me. I hadn't played well, so I knew what I was about to hear.

"Son." He said. "A lesser man would have screamed at the referee today and he would have been sent off." He took my hand and gave it a shake. "I am very proud of you for not losing your head and putting the team first."

I smiled sadly. "But boss, we lost. It made no difference."

He shook his head quickly. "Yes, but there'll be plenty of other chances for you to find glory. Be patient." He winked and wandered off to console our goalkeeper.

I learned a valuable lesson that day. Put your team first. Ignore the outside distractions. Be patient.

We had lost the Continental Cup - but the World Cup was still up for grabs. And that's where we were heading to next.

Go to page 106

CHAPTER 31

WITH ZHIVEC GONE TO MILANO AND A SUCCESSFUL first season behind me, I started my second season at Westfalen as the number one pick in the team. Our main rivals Bayer Monchen had signed some of the world's best players, including snatching our captain Maro Ruiz from us - it was going to be a challenge to keep the title and compete for the League Cup and European Cup as well that season. The money from the Ruiz transfer and the wages freed up from Zhivec's departure meant there was money for us to sign some players, which we did. A crop of exciting young players arrived, giving a fresh new dynamic to the team. It was an exciting place to be and I made sure to be as encouraging as possible to those new recruits.

We started the season in great form. I was in the best shape of my life, but we were lacking some of the star quality our main rivals at Bayer Monchen had recruited. It hurt to see our ex-captain Maro Ruiz in excellent form for them as well.

Approaching the season's midpoint and winter

break, we were still in both cups, but we were third in the league, with Bayer seven points clear at the top of the table. What's more, Monz FC was having an unexpected but excellent first half of the season and were two points ahead of us in second.

Fittingly, our final game before the mid-season break was against Monz FC. A win would put us above them and just within reach of Bayer, but a defeat would see us cut further adrift from the top two.

It had been a terrible game of soccer. We just hadn't clicked, and against a side in the form of Monz FC, we were always going to be punished. The surprise package of the season were playing some fantastic free-flowing soccer.

I knew, as well as the rest of the team, that no matter how well we were playing, it would be no excuse to our fans, who expected higher standards from us, as did our coach. We lost the game 3-0. I had the chance to pull one back in the 90th minute but uncharacteristically missed, hitting the post before the Monz FC goalkeeper calmly collected the ball. It had really been an awful game, and the winter break and Christmas with my family couldn't come soon enough. Losing 3-0 against an unestablished team like FC Monz just wasn't supposed to happen to Westfalen. The negativity around the club was compounded by the fact that the result saw Monz FC pull five points ahead of us in second place. Our standards were higher than that, and we all knew the coach would have something to say about it after the game.

Something had shifted recently. I had cemented my place as a first team player for one of the biggest clubs in Germany and Europe, wearing the famous number 10 jersey vacated by the great Ratan Zhivec. I had become incredibly popular inside Germany, and my star status was growing domestically as well as outside of the country.

I had some great individual performances in the European Cup, including a brace against one of, if not the, biggest club in the world, FC Catalonia. I was still young and felt like I had the world at my feet. My performances were consistently very good, and media endorsements and sponsorships had started rolling in. But something had been off lately with the coach and the way he talked to me. Perhaps it was the persistent rumors of a move to FC Catalonia that kept being circulated, or perhaps it was my growing media status outside of soccer that meant I hadn't been offered a new deal at Westfalen yet. That was despite still being on a comparatively low-wage contract. It certainly couldn't be my performances, could it?

I always hated the locker rooms after a defeat, as rare as that was at Westfalen. It always felt like a funeral. As we sat waiting in a somber silence for the coach, each player deep in their thoughts, I nudged my teammate Sanchez. He had signed for Westfalen on the same day as me. We had become good friends. He had only recently broken into the first team but had missed a couple of great chances with the game still level. "You're in for it, mate. The coach is really angry out there. He's going to have something to say about that sitter you missed at 0-0." Sanchez had been playing well recently, but the coach was never one to let young players get ahead of themselves or get too cocky. He liked to be firm but usually fair. "You're probably right, bro, but you hardly covered yourself in glory out there," came his reply.

With that, the door flung open. The coach stormed in, jersey sleeves rolled up and a face like thunder. I had seen him angry before, but this was different. I took a deep breath and gulped. "You, you useless waste of space," he was straight into Morty Hammels, our center back and now captain, a first-choice international for the German national team and one of the leading personalities in our dressing room. He was in no mood to hold back. "Let me see your cleats. Have you got concrete blocks in them or just cotton between your ears? You didn't want to track back, didn't want to mark their striker. What did you fancy doing out there today? Anything at all?! I'd rather have had my grandma out there; you were useless. You're dropped and training with the second team from now on." Hammels opened his mouth to reply but thought better of it, leaving him literally open-mouthed as the coach moved on to his next target.

The coach was spitting now, froth accumulating in the corners of his mouth, his thick-rimmed oval glasses steaming up as he pointed at Sanchez. Just as I had expected, he let a torrent of abuse out on him, "And you! I could have scored that chance. Shall I start myself ahead of you next week, you useless lump?" I nudged him in the ribs as if to say, 'I told you so, mate.'

The coach then turned to me. I could see the long

purple vein in his head throbbing, and his face turned a deeper shade of scarlet. I swallowed hard, immediately regretting what I had just done. "And what might be so funny," he was almost sneering now, venomous, with what felt like utter hatred spewing from his tightly wound face. "What would the star of the media's eye have to say about my soccer team?"

He was charging toward me now, finger pointing right at me, expletives tumbling from his mouth. He stopped just short of me and kicked out at a pile of jerseys on the floor, and as he did, he sent a soccer boot flying through the air right into my face. I held my hand up to my forehead - blood, blood gushing down my face.

In what was perhaps not the wisest move of my career, I saw red, jumping up to confront him, pointing at him and trying to get in his face. I was angry; I wanted to hit him, to tell him to back off. Did he not know who I was? Did he not realize the power I had over the media and the fans around here? My heart was pounding.

Our captain Hammels was the first to react, grabbing me and pulling me away as our Belgian midfielder Alex Wassel stepped between us. Things quickly de-escalated, but the damage was done. On my way out of the locker room, the coach stared at me and said nothing. It was the scariest look I'd ever been given.

I lay awake that night. I could never sleep after a defeat, but this was bigger than that. I went over the incident again and again in my head. At 6am, my phone lit up; it was my agent. "We need to talk about FC Catalonia."

My agent was clear, "Catalonia want you, they love you, they want to make you part of a team of world superstars that they are assembling, and they want to take advantage of the fact that your contract is up at the end of next season. They want to get you for a cut-price deal, and they want you *now*. They don't want to wait. But you'll have to force the move if you want to make it happen."

I knew I had the perfect ammunition to force a move. I could leak to the press what had just happened with the manager cutting my forehead open and try to force a move out of the club. Alternatively, I could stay, apologize, probably play a few second team games, and carry on playing for the team I love, where I've had so much success already.

DECISION TIME

If you decide to try and force a move, go to page 47

If you decide to stay, apologize, and fight for your place, go to page 104

CHAPTER 32

"♫ These are The Champions, Die Mester, Die Beste, Le Grandes Équipes, The Champions♫ "

I felt like I wanted to sing those lyrics at the top of my lungs as I lined up for Catalonia in the semi-final of the Champions League against London Blues. I'd been listening to that song every Tuesday and Wednesday night of my life wishing I'd be playing soccer in Europe. And now it was *finally* happening!

It's my first European start, and a final with Westfalen FC is at stake. I'm so glad I haven't told anyone about my niggly hamstring as my manager would have definitely benched me for this game if he had known.

As I shake hands with London Blues captain, Jay Perry, the enormity of the occasion hits me. I've just signed my first professional contract and I'm *one* game away from the biggest soccer game in club competition.

The manager has moved Bobaldinho to play on

the right wing, and accommodated me on the left. Impressive tactics, given a lot of the press were saying we couldn't play in the same team as we were both left wingers. Little did they know that now we posed a double threat.

⚽ ⚽ ⚽

We're under constant pressure from London Blues for the first 15 minutes of the game, and I've not had a touch of the ball. It's not until they miskick a corner that Bobaldinho picks the ball up and gives me the eyes.

I can see that there's nothing but green grass between me and the London Blue's keeper - all their defenders had gone up to try and score from their corner.

Bobaldinho pumps a perfect ball into the opposition half and I know I'm in. I know I'll score if I get to it, so, like a greyhound out of the traps, I explode into a powerful run to meet Bobaldinho's pass.

BANG! Agony! I clutch my leg as I collapse to the ground screaming in pain. The loud bang I've just heard is the sound of my hamstring snapping as I tried to chase the ball.

"Kiddo, you'll be fine. We've got the best doctors in the business." The manager tells me gently, as I'm stretchered off the ground.

I can feel the tears roll down my cheek as I cover my face with my hands. It's not so much the pain in my leg but the realization that I'm going to miss the Champions League final in two weeks time.

⚽ ⚽ ⚽

It's a tough walk up the stadium stairs to collect my Champions League winning medal.

We have beaten Westfalen 2-1 in the Champions League final.

It is a tough walk not because I'm struggling to get the hang of these crutches, but because the truth is that I'd much rather have played in this game. Even if we had lost!

"Congratulations to the man of the hour!" Says an important looking man in a suit as I stumble on my crutches up the stairs in the stadium.

"Thank you," I reply with a big smile, hoping that my acting skills don't betray my *real* feelings.

He obviously knows nothing about soccer. How can I be a "man of the hour" when I didn't even play?!

The President of EUFA puts a winner's medal around my neck, but I quickly take it off and tightly clench it in my hand. I take one last look at my teammates dancing and parading the trophy around the stadium and decide it's enough. It hurts too much to watch them celebrating having not contributed in the game.

I go into the dressing room by myself and decide to focus on my next big goal, being fit for the World Cup which begins in Germany in only a few weeks' time.

Go to page 25

CHAPTER 33

We were flying on a wave of positivity and were ready to take the game to Bayer Monchen… but the Germans were ready for us.

Tancker forced a fantastic save from Smike within the first minute of the second half. A quick slap in the face, dragging us back to reality.

Monchen maintained their control of the game for the next 20 minutes, forcing Sir Alec to bring on Teddingham up front. He quickly changed the shape of the game, giving us a new lease of life. With our goalkeeper proving a force of nature between the sticks, we had the confidence to take the game to the Germans.

With 10 minutes to go, Sir Alec went for broke and subbed on Oli for Andy to join Teddingham up front. Within his first minute, the young Scandinavian found space in the box, connecting with a diving header from my cross. It was almost an instant impact, but the Monchen keeper saved it.

We could smell fear.

I checked the stadium clock, five minutes of standard time left. I looked back, just in time to see the Monchen keeper punt a goal kick aimlessly into the middle of the field. Buoyed with a second wind, I charged toward the falling ball and won the header, knocking it out wide to Beckenham. He coolly took it in his stride and responded to a shout from Teddingham, who had made a quick run into the box. Beckenham passed into Teddingham's stride, who swiped it goal-bound. SAVE.

The Germans weren't going down without a fight but boy were we ready for it.

The crowd roared as the fourth official flashed an extra three minutes of added time on the board. Three minutes. 180 seconds to steal victory from the jaws of defeat. Surely it was now impossible to win, but we could at least get a draw and take it to extra-time.

Every attack was now a long ball into the Monchen penalty area; hoping for a mistake that we could pounce on. In the 89th minute, our full back Denny Birwin won a corner after a lovely bit of skill from Beckenham.

Beckenham looked up at me, "You want this or shall I?" He's visibly exhausted and doubting himself.

DECISION TIME

If you grab the ball and take the corner yourself, go to page 149

If you let Beckenham take the corner, go to page 159

CHAPTER 34

It was a tight-knit locker room at Westfalen, and there was no reason for any of this to go any further if I didn't bring attention to it. Looking in the mirror, I made sure to conceal the cut with some makeup and wore my long hair down over my forehead.

As soon as I pulled up at training, my teammate Sanchez was straight onto me. "You're in for it today mate. The coach is going to tear you apart for what happened after the Monz game. You'll be joining me in the second team, and that's if you're lucky. And what's this about FC Catalonia? You better not be thinking of leaving us, of leaving me, your friend?!"

I laughed; it felt good to laugh after the last few days. "Come on... it was nothing... it'll be alright... won't it?" Just as Sanchez went to reply, he was interrupted by Hammels, who suddenly appeared out of nowhere from behind us. "...You're wanted in the coach's office... now..."

"Sit down, *boy*." The coach was already sitting behind his large wooden desk, peering at me over his thick-rimmed glasses. The walls were covered in pictures of him with some of the game's greats, and newspaper articles of cup wins, league wins, and individual honors adorned the shelves that lined the room's walls. Careers had been made and lost in this room, and you could feel the weight of it around the place.

"What have you got to say for yourself, then, *boy*?" I'd noticed the manager often called players 'boy' when he was pulling rank, but this was no time to talk back to him. Sheepishly, I looked up at him, made eye contact, the words briefly sticking in my throat. "I'm sorry, boss. It won't happen again, boss." He sat back, pausing for what felt like an age. He put his hands together in a point, leaning forward. "You're absolutely right - it won't ever happen again."

The words were so simple but delivered in such a way that I knew I'd never talk back to him again.

The next day, the chairman called me in with a new five-year contract offer, and I knew I'd be staying at Westfalen.

Go to page 10

CHAPTER 35

Our first game in Dubai was against Saudi Arabia. The UAE World Cup was kicking off with us as joint favorites to win it, alongside the French.

"BOYS, in a huddle now!" The players stopped doing their last minute stretches on the field and jogged over. As they gathered around me, I was surprised that they even heard me. The Saudis had brought so many fans across the border that the stadium was overflowing with them. Saudi Arabian fans were some of the loudest fans I had ever heard!

"Listen up. This is the beginning of the end!" I said enthusiastically. "And the end is taking this trophy back home and back to our loved ones. Let's go!"

"LET'S GO!" They all shouted back in unison.

⚽ ⚽ ⚽

"We'll turn things around, trust me. As captain, I'll make sure that happens", I said to the Channel 1 reporter after she'd asked if our World Cup was over.

In what could only be described as the upset of the century, the Saudis had beaten us 2-1. Talk of our World Cup being over was nonsense though. I was the best player on the planet and I wasn't planning on leaving the world stage with a whimper.

I put my arm around each of the boys after the game and guaranteed them we would turn things around. And together, through sheer hard work, that is *exactly* what we started to do.

First against the Mexicans, where I scored one and set one up for Lopatoni. We ruthlessly dispatched them 2-0. I was in no mood to mess about.

Then against the Polish, who had the world's best striker at the time, Dewanloski, firing on all cylinders. Our defenders did really well to keep him quiet, and we again scored two goals on the counter attack to beat them 2-0.

We were through to the knockout stages and up against the Australians. They have never been a powerhouse of soccer, but what they lack in talent they make up for in industry, athleticism and hard work! We ground out a 2-1 victory against the Aussies, and it took a lovely solo effort from me to finally break them down.

In the Quarter Finals we drew The Netherlands of Dick Van Virg. Needless to say, there was still a lot of bad blood between the two teams after we had eliminated them in the semi-finals in Brazil a few years back.

In an effort to destabilize me and the team, Van Virg and their new manager Davi Advocaat had said in all their recent press conferences how unsporting we *all* were. I would be having none of that!

The Dutch started ferociously, a few dirty challenges left our winger Di Martini needing treatment for a gash on his leg that ran from his knee to the top of his ankle. The referee didn't even book the Dutch player for that and a huge fight broke out.

It was clear that the Dutch weren't here to play soccer - they were here for a physical battle.

I scored the only goal of the game and immediately ran to the halfway line to celebrate in front of Advocaat. I cupped my ears in my hands and stared him in the face as the roar of our fans filled the stadium.

Onto the semi-finals we progressed. Watching the news was mind-blowing. People in our home country were selling their houses just to be able to buy plane tickets to the UAE and watch us in person.

The momentum within our camp was growing, we comfortably beat Croatia 3-0 in the semi-final to set up a date with destiny.

Everything I had ever worked for in my life came down to the 90 minutes ahead. 90 minutes which were going to be played the following Sunday in a state of the art stadium in the heart of a Middle Eastern desert.

⚽ ⚽ ⚽

My heart couldn't stop beating. It was almost as if it was going to burst out of my chest. I tried to sing the national anthem louder to see if that would help, but the truth is our 40,000 fans in the stadium were drowning me out.

I had never experienced such passion, such anticipation. This final against France meant *everything* for *everyone* back home.

"Good luck and may the best man win," I said to Kyle Mtakke, the French captain and one of the best players in the world, as we lined up for the customary pre-game handshakes.

"GUYS, HUDDLE NOW!"

As my teammates jogged towards me, it struck me how young they all were. It was there and then that my age dawned on me. I was 35 and I would never have the opportunity to play in a World Cup *ever* again..

"Boys, it's now or never. It's on us to write our own life stories. Are you ready to become soccer IMMORTALS?!"

"YEEEEAHHHH!!" came back their rousing response.

As I looked around at the 10 faces of my teammates, I realized they admired me. I was to them what Bobaldinho had been to me 20 years earlier.

"Captain, you single-handedly got me into soccer. I was born on the day you made your debut for FC Catalonia." Monty Gonzales, one of the youngest members of our squad, said. His eyes were locked on me.

"It is an honor to go out there with you and bring this trophy back to our people. I will give my all to you today, Skipper!"

"You inspire us all, every day, Captain. And you have done so for the last 20 years," said Julio Alvaron.

"And today, it's on us to pay *you* back." He said before breaking off the huddle with a big "LET'S GO!!"

The boys did indeed inspire me!

We battered the French in the first half, and within 36 minutes we were 2-0 up. I was playing well and scored the first goal of the game through a penalty.

The half-time talk from the manager was to keep doing what we were doing. So off we went to play the second half, knowing that we were only 45 minutes away from winning the World Cup!

I looked up at the stadium screen to see what was on the clock. 10 minutes remaining before we'd be crowned World Champions.

No one can turn around a 2-0 deficit in 10 minutes. Surely not, especially not the way we're playing. That just doesn't happen in soccer, least of all in a final of a World Cup.

Unfortunately, Kyle Mtakke had different plans. Setting a captain's example, he single-handedly demolished our defense in two horrific minutes.

He won a penalty and scored it in the 81st minute, and just 60 seconds later, he latched onto a through-ball from French stalwart Tiezzman and volleyed it first-time into the bottom of the net.

That was a hammer blow to my heart. I was nine minutes away from winning the World Cup and Kyle Mtakke had taken it away from me… for now.

I saw my teammates' heads go down, their shoulders started to slump.

"BOYS! HEADS UP *NOW*! WE ARE NOT LOSING SO DON'T ACT LIKE WE ARE!"

It worked. I saw them arch their backs. I needed them to know that it was far from over. And that I was going to bring this trophy back home. Even if I had to do it *all* by myself.

⚽⚽⚽

"You already had the win in the palm of your hands. Now go out there and do it again!" The manager said to us as we were getting ready for the first half of extra-time.

"You haven't come this far to go home empty handed. Let's bring it back home!"

⚽⚽⚽

In 20 years of playing professional soccer at the highest level, I never saw anything that resembled the following 30 minutes.

22 of the best players in the world giving their all to score a goal. No one wanted this game to go to penalties. There was too much at stake. It was an end-to-end soccer battle of the highest calibre, being played in front of 80,000 people, and being broadcast live to more than *one billion* people across the globe.

In one of our counter attacks, Julio Alvaron found himself open on the edge of the 6-yard box and smashed the hardest kick of a ball ever seen across the goalkeeper. The French number one somehow managed to get a palm to it, but the ricochet fell at my feet.

I kicked the ball toward the empty net only to see

a French defender clear it. But the defender was a yard behind the line. *Behind* the line. That means the ball had undoubtedly crossed the line and the VAR technology would prove it.

I didn't wait for VAR, I ran to the sidelines and celebrated my goal. Surely *NOW* we had won it!

The stadium erupted into mayhem. Our fans were deafening. My teammates engulfed me in a wave of happiness.

"Skipper. You've done it! YEAHHHHHHHHH!!!" Alvaron shouted in my face as he clasped it firmly in his hands.

I had scored two goals in a World Cup final. I knew it was coming home, but I didn't know I'd play *such* an influential role in the final.

We were 12 minutes away from securing the most coveted of trophies.

However, *yet again*, Mtakke had different ideas as to how this night would pan out. And *he* wanted to be the most influential player of the final.

With two minutes of the game remaining he won a penalty.

30 seconds later, and seemingly with ice running through his veins, he converted that penalty. The guy had just scored a *hat-trick* in a world cup final and had broken our hearts yet again.

"Maybe it isn't meant to be," I started thinking. "Maybe I'm destined to never win the greatest trophy that there is to win."

As these negative thoughts were invading my head, I saw a French player break through our line of defense. He was one-on-one with Dubi, our goal-keeper. My heart dropped.

This was well and truly game over.

The French striker smashed the ball toward the bottom corner of the net only for Dubi to stick his leg out, more in hope than anything else. The ball struck his leg and went flying into the stands. He had just pulled off the most incredible save ever seen in a World Cup final!

"C'mon, Skipper. Heads up! It's not over yet!" He shouted at me.

That woke me from my slumber. It really was time to step up…

PEEEEP PEEEEP PEEEEEEEEEEEEEEP!

The referee blew for full-time.

My date with destiny was to be decided on penalties.

I placed the ball on the spot, feeling the weight of the world on my shoulders.

As I stepped back, memories of my childhood flooded my mind —

My dad struggling to pay for my growth hormone treatment.

The countless hours spent perfecting my free kick technique as other teammates went out partying.

My parents living in separate countries so that I could play for a European team.

Overcoming being a shy teenager.

Moving to a new country.

Winning countless tournaments.

All the dreams that had fueled my journey to this *very* moment, had come true at some point or another in my life. All apart from one. Winning the World

Cup. And here I was, moments away from making this *one last dream* come true…

With a deep breath, I ran toward the ball, pouring every ounce of skill, prowess and determination into the strike. The ball soared into the top corner, beyond the reach of the despairing goalkeeper. We were one-up, and it was now time for the boys to complete the job.

Mtakke obviously scored his penalty to equalize for the French, but after that Dubi made sure that no other ball was going to get past him in the shoot out.

Dubi saved the second French penalty. And then the third.

My teammates and I embraced in a hug in the center circle as Dubi pulled off save after save. He'd lock eyes after each save and point at me, mouthing the words, *"we've got this, captain."*

After a few kicks it came down to Monty Gonzales to take his penalty.

If he scored, we won. Simple as that.

As he walked from the center circle to the penalty spot, his pre-match words kept echoing in my head;

"I was born on the day you made your debut for FC Catalonia."

He turned his head as he walked to the ball and gave me a short nod. The sort of nod that re-assured me that he had this. If he was nervous, he most definitely wasn't showing it.

"You single-handedly got me into soccer," his words continued to echo through my head.

He placed the ball on the spot.

"You inspired me to keep playing this sport."

He took three steps back and made his run towards the ball.

We all held our breath as he struck the ball with his instep. It flew into the top right corner of the net.

The ground beneath me started shaking. Chaos engulfed the stadium around us. I'd never witnessed scenes like this before - it was pandemonium from everyone in our team - absolute mayhem.

I got sucker punched by a feeling of relief - a feeling so strong that it brought me to my knees. It was on my knees that I started wailing uncontrollably - I just couldn't stop crying.

As I put my hands to my face I got embraced by a couple of my teammates.

"We did it! We did it, Skip! We're…" my teammates we're choking up too. The tears and the sobbing didn't allow them to finish the sentence.

Luckily for them, our physio finished the sentence for them as he threw himself on us in celebration.

"WE'RE WORLD CHAMPIONS, BABY! WOHOOOO!"

He kissed my cheek after he'd knocked me over. "Thank you, THANK YOU!!!"

I kissed his cheek back and immediately ran towards Dubi and Alavaron who were hugging near the corner flag. A sea of fans behind them were still leaping in ecstasy waving our national flag.

The noise around us reached unprecedented levels, I literally couldn't hear Dubi and Alvaron as we embraced each other. Dubi covered my ears to somewhat drown out the noise. He then shouted:

"We did it for you, Skipper. The world's best *ever* player deserves this trophy. This is all for *AND* because of you. Enjoy your moment!"

I looked up and saw 40,000 compatriots chanting my name. Adults were crying and strangers were hugging. I took a moment to myself to take it all in. My lifelong dream had *just* become a reality.

After the team had all collected their medals, it was down to me as captain to bring the trophy to them. We had done it. Against all odds, and despite Mtakke having the best individual performance a World Cup final had ever seen, we had won the World Cup.

As I got handed my winner's medal I took a step towards it: The one trophy that had eluded me in 20 years of playing soccer. It was a thing of beauty.

The trophy shimmered brightly in my hands, a testament to years of dedication, sacrifice and unwavering belief. I held it aloft in front of my teammates and the fireworks went off, we had officially been crowned World Champions. I could barely see my teammates' faces as the confetti showered us from the heavens.

My teammates placed me on their shoulders as I paraded the World Cup trophy around the stadium to the fans. It was a perfect fit. Despite the heavy weight, the trophy nestled snugly in my hands. As I continued to hear 40,000 fans chant my name in unison, I couldn't help but feel humbled by the journey that had led me to this glorious moment - and as if by magic, the two people who had made it possible for me were lifted high alongside me.

I found myself celebrating with my mom and dad who, 20 years earlier had given everything up for me. This was *their* victory as much as it was mine.

In that stadium, on that starry night in Dubai, I etched my name into the annals of world soccer. I had made history. I had become the player who defied all limitations to emerge victorious. The man who inspired a generation of soccer players in my country to win the greatest trophy of them all.

The World Cup was now ours, and, as I was carried off on the shoulders of my teammates back to our dressing room, it dawned on me that I would be forever remembered as the undisputed G.O.A.T.

AND JUST LIKE THAT, I BECAME THE GREATEST OF ALL ***Time.***

CHAPTER 36

I DIDN'T WANT TO RUN AWAY AND FORCE A MOVE, THAT wasn't how I was brought up. Just imagining my mom's face on finding out I'd driven to Manchester was scary enough.

"I've got an idea." I said to my agent. "I know Lilywhites want to keep me, but what about if we negotiate? Try to get the club as much money as possible." He frowned at me for a second, but that quickly turned into a smile.

"I like your ambition kid. These opportunities don't come up very often."

We walked back to the chairwoman and followed her through her enormous house, into her huge garden.

"Right, let's get this deal sorted, shall we?" She said, already handing me a pen and showing me the contract on the table.

I didn't move. Neither did my agent. "Erm, what's wrong here?" Asked the chairwoman. I shifted uncomfortably in my seat, waiting for my agent to do what he's paid to do.

"Manchester." He started. "They want to make a bid for the kid."

She had turned from grinning Cheshire cat to an ice cold statue. This wasn't going to be easy.

"We want him to stay, and we want him to take the iconic number 10." She said very directly to me, catching my eye and holding it in her hands. "Manchester are a rival club, and I can't in all good conscience hand over our best player."

She was still staring into my soul. As much as it was nice to be called that, her eye-contact was beginning to give me the creeps.

"You and the club have been really great to me." I meant it. "Amazing actually." I added. "But this is a once in a lifetime offer and I can't pretend it doesn't exist. I could have tried to force a move and disrespected you, but I didn't. I'm here, wanting to talk."

She shifted in her seat a little uncomfortably, I think my words had gotten through that icy skin.

"Well, I can only accept £50,000,000 for a player of your potential and as far as I know, Manchester won't pay more than £30,000,000. Sorry." She stated, a little more warmly than before.

My agent cleared his throat and joined the conversation again. "Well, I've just had a text from big red Sir Alec, the Manchester manager. We go way back," he smiled. "He wants to speak to you."

He handed his phone to the chairwoman, which immediately started ringing. A little surprised, she flipped open the phone, "Hello Sir Alec. What a surprise."

My agent turned and smiled at me. He knew something I didn't. The phone conversation continued, but we could only hear one side of it.

"Right, okay, I didn't know that..." The chairwoman responded, waiting for a response. "Yes, that's the price. Not a penny less." She wasn't budging.

She smiled, not an overly happy one but still confident.

"Okay. Send the paperwork and we can get this moving." She was quiet again as Sir Alec spoke. "Yes, I do. It's still parked out the front." She laughed. "Yeah, of course you can. Pop round whenever you like, you're welcome to give it a drive." She closed the phone, ending the call.

"Never had him down as a fan of pink." She chuckled.

Looking at my agent and then back to me, the chairwoman sighed. "It's done. You're a Manchester player. Thank you for your honesty and your loyalty to the club. We'll all remember you fondly."

Wow. I had just become a Manchester Devils player.

Go to page 153

CHAPTER 37

In my head, the Manchester jersey was back on! I turned, got into my car and sped away from the castle, past two turrets and a pink tank quicker than you could say "TRAITOR" ...and I had a feeling some people would.

RING RING. It was my agent.

"Okay, so you've made your move. I'll let Manchester know you're on your way. We have exactly four hours to get this contract signed. Or you stay at the club. A very angry club."

I could hear the chairwoman screaming in the background. I hoped for my agent's sake that she didn't have any swords or spears in that castle of hers.

I made it to Manchester with less than 30 minutes to go on transfer deadline day. But as I pulled into the training ground, rather than a welcome party, there was no one.

My phone rang. It was my agent.

"Hey kid. So, we have a slight issue...the chair-woman was so mad at you that she called

Manchester and told them that there was no way she was selling you to them in a million years." I felt like crying. "She then threw her phone at me and told me that you're going nowhere. You've got three years left on your contract and you're playing every minute of it rotting in Lilywhites' second team."

I hit the steering wheel in anger. What had I done?!

"I'm afraid there aren't going to be any premier league clubs coming in for you either. You're going to have to take a step down and prove yourself again." He sounded sad.

AND JUST LIKE THAT MY SOCCER CAREER ENDED.

CHAPTER 38

I can't believe it's been a whole year since I joined the Jewels Old Boys Academy. And what a year it has been!

I was completely taken aback by the quality of soccer here! I went from always being the best player on the field to… well, I'm still the best player but it's not as easy as it used to be back home. It's like they 'get' soccer a lot more here, which makes it a bit harder to get past defenders. But only ever so slightly.

Despite being by far the best player on the field every time we play, there's been something that has been troubling my mom and dad, and that's my height.

Whilst all my teammates have rocketed in height in the last 12 months, I remain quite short. I'll be honest, it does make me feel a bit left out, but as long as I'm playing better than them out on the field, it doesn't really matter.

My dad, however, seems super worried. So much so that we're both currently waiting at the doctor's office to get back results from a test I did three weeks ago.

"You may go in now," says the receptionist as Dad uncomfortably rushes us in to see the Doctor.

⚽⚽⚽

"Growth hor... WHAT?!" I'm sure I look perplexed as I stare into Dad's eyes. Is he even talking to me in English?

"Growth hormone deficiency, son. It just means that you will *always* be shorter than everyone else."

"But..." I really start to worry now. I had been looking forward to growing up and being taller than everyone. That was always going to make me an *even* better soccer player.

"But... surely there's a way around it, Dad?"

"I'm afraid there isn't, son." Dad says somberly. "The pills to make you grow taller are too expensive for your mom and I to afford."

"But isn't this the same problem that my cousin Albe had in Spain?" I say optimistically. "He got his soccer club to pay for the pills"

"That's true." Dad responds, his head and posture finally picking up slightly.

"We could go to Spain and try and get a trial for you to play at FC Catalonia. If they like how you play they could maybe pay for your treatment. I know you're good enough to shine in Spain son, the only thing is we'd be risking all our life savings and they could choose to not *even* see you play!"

"If you stay here at Jewels Old Boys you can keep progressing through the ranks and see how it goes... what would you rather do?"

DECISION TIME

If you go to Spain on the off chance that FC Catalonia will give you a trial, go to page 15

If you stay playing your soccer at Jewels Old Boys, go to page 161

CHAPTER 39

I FLOATED THE BALL, CURLING IT OVER THE GOALKEEPER to sit perfectly for Conaldo to head. He charged with grace, leaping and gliding through the air like a majestic eagle over a calm valley. He was about a foot above any Gunnerbury player and neatly used his head to tuck the ball into the back of their net.

YES! 2-2. We were back in the game.

I turned and caught a look at Sir Alec. I was hoping I'd changed his half-time plans of screaming at me in-front of the whole team and coaching squad. He saw me and raised a thumb. Phew!

The whistle blew. Half-time. Everything to play for.

Go to page 127

CHAPTER 40

The manager made two subs at the break, moving me into the middle of the field and adding an extra striker up top. We weren't giving up this chance. Time to take the brakes off.

Within four minutes we were 3-2 up. A lovely team goal that saw every player touch the ball before it hit the Gunnerbury net. We smelt blood in the water, and we weren't going to let go until we'd all been fed.

I was having a great game now. Gunnerbury's midfield couldn't cope with us. Skols was passing them off the park and Beano wasn't letting a single player have more than a second on the ball. It was this relentless tackling and forward passing that got me my first goal of the game.

Beano won a header that landed right at my feet and without thinking, I knocked it past two Gunnerbury defenders and hit the ball first-time into the bottom corner.

4-2. The league title was increasingly looking like it was ours.

The fans believed it too. Delighting in chanting 'Champions of England, you'll never sing that' to the disappointed away fans. I shared a quiet smile, not wanting to gloat.

The next 25 minutes saw us score three more goals. Conaldo was having a field day coming in from the left and skinning defenders with his quick feet. He'd scored a hat-trick already.

7-2. What a way to win a league title.

But the soccer Gods were not quite done yet. With one minute to go, Conaldo was brought down outside the box 20 yards from the Gunnerbury goal. He took our free-kicks, no one even dared question that status quo.

However, for some reason he called my name and ushered me over. "Amigo, take it home." He said, handing me the ball. I gave him a confused look. "I insist. I've got three today, I'm taking that ball home with me. I can let you play with it for another few minutes." He added, smiling.

I nodded and whispered in his ear. "How about that thing we were trying in training?" He laughed and shrugged. "Sure thing, amigo. I got you."

Conaldo stood over the ball, the Gunnerbury players expecting him to take the kick. But we had other plans.

He stepped to the ball, scooped it up with his laces and stepped back; leaving me with the space to try something I'd never attempted in a competitive game. A standing scissor-kick…from 20 yards out!

The ball flew off my boot directly toward the Gunnerbury goal. Their goalkeeper had to change direction and scrambled across the line to get near it, but he couldn't. It smashed the underside of the bar and bounced into the net.

The stadium went NUTS. Full, no-holds barred craziness! The players chased me as I ran off to the Drestford End of the stadium, all piling in on me in celebration. Sir Alec was dancing. Well, it looked like dancing, but not a dance I'd ever seen before.

The referee blew the final whistle, putting Gunnerbury out of their misery and placing the League medals around our necks.

We'd done it. We'd won the league.

DECISION TIME

FC Catalonia have never stopped following your career. After this incredible league win, they contact Manchester Devils and offer a world-record transfer fee for you. If you decide to join Catalonia FC, go to page 136

Sir Alec is desperate to keep you and offers you a new contract making you the highest paid player at the club. He wants you to stay and help the club win a Champions League title next season. If you decide to stay, go to page 131

CHAPTER 41

Now wasn't the time to be greedy. I hadn't played enough minutes for my legs to be warm enough to try a 25 yard screamer from a dead ball.

I raised both arms, indicating that the ball was going to the back post and hit the inside of my foot across the ball, to curl it goal-bound and into our strikers.

The ball was good, but our striker's runs were not. The opposition goalkeeper, jumping high to catch the ball, buried it in his arms and fell to the ground to waste time.

The referee blew his whistle, ending the game and my last chance for international success. It has been an incredible ride but deep down I knew I'd always wonder 'What if I'd taken the shot for myself?'.

And just like that my soccer career ended.

CHAPTER 42

WHAT A SUMMER. THE LEAGUE CELEBRATIONS WERE incredible. We sailed a sea of red, black and white through the streets of Manchester on an open-top bus. Even Sir Alec was smiling!

A week after the celebrations, Sir Alec flew my entire family over to the city to witness me signing my new contract with Manchester Devils. My mom was beaming with pride and was even given her own Manchester jersey with my name and number on the back. She barely took it off the entire trip!

But that was last year and we're well into another successful season.

Sir Alec gave us all the rather difficult task of winning THE TREBLE – the League title, the Cup and the Champions League – all in one season. "It's never been done before lads," he chuckled. I'd laugh if I thought he was saying it in jest. I knew he knew we could do it.

Belief is a funny thing and a man like Sir Alec drills it into you like a nail into wood. "Son, with feet like tha' and a brain ta' match, yaw gonna bag us a whole lotta' goals." That's what he told me down the tunnel before our first game of the season and he wasn't wrong.

Come the last game of the season I had scored 28 goals and assisted 17 times… and with only one league game to go, I got treble fever.

⚽⚽⚽

Match Day.

Inspired by my mate Conaldo, who had sadly left for Madrid White in the summer, I arrived at the home of the Manchester Devils early, as he always used to do, to soak up the day and settle my mind into game mode. Elite soccer wasn't just about skill; mentally preparing myself was important as well.

Sir Alec had really created a fantastic family atmosphere at the stadium. Everyone knew everyone; whether you were the uniform man, worked in the club shop, or wore the number one jersey playing in goal, you could stop and have a chat with anyone. I loved it.

Everyone was excited. With one game to go, we needed three points to win the league and put a stop to any chance Gunnerbury might have had of getting their hands on silverware.

Sir Alec had the words THE TREBLE in bold, printed and stuck above the door in the home locker room – our goal was clear. It was time to bring home the trophy and retain it for Manchester.

The stadium was pumping as we kicked off. You could feel the fans' excitement. It felt like ours. But that proved a mistake. We started slowly, allowing the London Lilywhites time on the ball and plenty of chances at goal. Our Danish goalkeeper, Peter Smike, screamed from the very depths of his throat at our defense, midfield, and attack... everyone. Even the referee.

I was playing in center midfield, pushed forward to attack and supply the ball to our strikers. Well, that was the plan, but I wasn't receiving it anywhere near enough. I dropped back to pick the ball up in our own half, and in my desperation to get forward, placed a poor pass behind Skols in the middle.

The Lilywhites' skillful midfielder Aaron Manderton jumped on my mistake and hit a first-time, outside-of-the-boot curled pass onto the feet of their striker Big Les, who took one touch and smashed it past Peter in our goal.

We were behind and it was my fault.

I didn't dare catch a glance over at Sir Alec. By then, I knew his reactions off by heart and didn't need to catch a death stare. I knew what I needed to do.

Beano called everyone into a huddle before we kicked off. "Stupid mistake." He had his hand on my shoulder a little more firmly than I would have liked. "...But we move on." He then stared directly at me. "You attackers better pull your fingers out, it's all very well scoring all season, but if you fail to do it now, it means nothing."

He barked a guttural war-cry. Sure, it was terrifying, but we all knew what he meant.

It didn't take long to draw level. Our superstar right midfielder Javid Beckenham used his magic wand of a right foot to drill a low shot across the goal into the far corner. We all ran straight back to the center spot, no nonsense.

The job wasn't done yet.

Half-time came and went. We were all over them for the next 40 minutes. Our cultured defenders played neat passes into the midfield, Skolsy never took more than two touches to move the ball quickly into attack, every pass was perfect. The only thing missing was a shot on target, and the crowd was getting anxious.

I heard Sir Alec from a distance. "Oi, ya' wee bugger. Stop that passing and take a shot." It could have been aimed at Skolsy, Beckenham, or me, but there was something in the way he said it that felt personal.

The Lilywhites were panicking. We had moved further up the field and were pressing them in. Skols drilled a ball at me across the center of the field and screamed, "do something, mate!"

I took a quick first touch out of my feet and lifted my head. The best players always gave themselves a second to assess their options, and two options very quickly opened up...

Our striker, Wight Dorke, had made a run to the back post beyond his defender and was waving his hand at me. All I needed to do was curl a pass into his run for him to nod home. Easy.

But in their caution, the Lilywhite midfield had dropped off, leaving me 10 yards of space around the edge of the box. I could try and do something magical.

. . .

DECISION TIME

If you decide to curl a pass to the back post, go to page 144

If you decide to try something magical, go to page 77

CHAPTER 43

It had been 10 months since my transfer to FC Catalonia and I was loving life in Spain! Perhaps it was because we'd been winning almost every game!

On a personal note, I felt like I owed much of my recent success to my national team manager. I could still hear his words echoing in my head after we'd lost to the Germans in last summer's World Cup: " Bottle this feeling. Remember how much you *hate* losing. Let it propel you to greatness, son."

"Everything you desire is within your reach, but *only* if you work hard at it."

Little did he know that I'd take every *single* word in to make sure I didn't lose again. Both on the international stage and at club level.

From my very first training session at FC Catalonia I knew I'd made the right choice to move! Not only was I playing with some of the best players in the world, the weather and the lifestyle suited me down to a tee. I missed my old team and my team-mates - but this was soccer and if I wanted to be the best then I needed to play with the best, and, at FC Catalonia that was certainly the case!

I hit the ground running and it felt like I'd been playing here for years, the way I was linking up with my teammates, it reminded me of my early days in soccer with my friend Gus! I was playing regularly and scoring a ton of goals too! And it wasn't long before I was lining up in the Champions League final with my new team. We were facing our arch domestic rivals Madrid White at England's famous Werberly stadium. We'd already beaten them to the league title and the domestic cup, and this was sure to be an explosive derby game with soccer greatness and pride on the line for both teams.

We went 1-0 down to a goal from a familiar face, Renato Conaldo scoring for Madrid with a powerful strike from distance. But that goal only had the effect of waking us up and soon we were pinging the ball around, moving into space and creating dangerous attacks from every angle. Madrid simply couldn't get hold of the ball as we played the most beautiful soccer the modern game had ever seen. So much so that it got its own name: Tiki-taka soccer. If I ever thought my connection with my childhood friend Gus was telepathic, then I really had no words for how I could read my teammates Xernandez and Aliesta. It was almost like we were the same person and we were *always* one step ahead of the opposition.

We ended up comfortably winning 3-1. I got the second goal of the game and was happy with my performance. It was always nice helping the team to greatness.

"Championeeee…Championneee.. Ole… Ole… Ole" we sang as we paraded the big-eared trophy around the London stadium. I wanted to keep dancing with my teammates when I got pulled away for a TV interview.

"How does it feel to have been immortalized in the history of this club? Do you realize you won *everything* you competed for this season? People are saying this is *THE* best team in the history of the sport. Would you agree?"

I froze. *'Wow'*.

It hadn't really hit me until then. We *had* won everything we competed for: The Opener Shield, The League, The Cup, The Super Cup, The World Club Cup and now The Champions League for the second time in two years.

"Yes. It's a testament to the hard work we've all put in," I said, trying to play it cool.

"If there are any young fans out there, I just want to say that everything you desire is within your reach, but *only* if you work hard at it." I said to the global TV cameras.

"And just lastly, before you go…" said the reporter. "Surely you think you're going to beat Renato Conaldo in next month's ceremony to decide who the best player on this planet is?"

It had been a few weeks since we'd won it all and I found myself sitting next to Conaldo in Zurich. FISA had made us sit together as it was clearly between him and me as to who was going to win the award for the best player on the planet. I think it made for some iconic viewing for audiences around the world.

I couldn't stop thinking about Mom and Dad at this stage. This nomination was really for them. All the sacrifices they made to get me to Spain as a young boy had enabled me to join this incredible team that was being touted as the best *ever*!

The beauty of this particular award, and the reason why I wanted to win it, is because it was voted for by your fellow professional players from around the world. Recognition from your peers is as high a praise as you can get.

"... and the winner is..."

Yet again I was stunned. They had just said my name. A flurry of emotions overcame my body. I felt a bit lightheaded as I walked to the stage to pick up my soccer shaped trophy.

As I did the customary meet and greet after giving my speech, I got approached by a man in a white robe.

"Al Bin Shaffa - pleased to make your acquaintance," he said with a heavy Arabic accent.

"I know the best player in the world will have little time at this event, so I'll make it brief," he said as we were shaking hands.

"The best player in the world deserves to have the best salary in the world. I want to offer you one million dollars a week to come and play for my team Al Qaffa." He barely paused.

"We'll pay Catalonia whatever they want for you. Money really is no issue - we want to make you the highest paid sports start in the history of the world. I just need a decision from you now."

. . .

DECISION TIME

If you decide that becoming the highest paid sports player in the history of the world is important to you, go to page 79

If you decide that, still in your 20s, you've got plenty of opportunity to improve as a player and your best place to do it at is Catalonia, go to page 35

CHAPTER 44

THE PAST YEAR'S BEEN GREAT AT THE CLAUDIUS REYNER Academy, I get to see most of my old friends, my family and I'm *easily* the best player here. Even Gus is here with me!

It's been great scoring goals for fun, and having Gus here means I'm never short on opportunities. I do wonder sometimes though…is this *too* easy? I mean, it's great being the best player on the field, but I do wonder if the other players here take it quite as seriously as me.

I've noticed recently that some of my teammates are rushing to leave training whilst I'm staying behind to practice free kicks, or they are turning up late when I'm always in early working on close control and shooting drills. Sometimes it can feel a little bit like I'm an outsider, like I'm the only one fully invested in improving my performances.

Even Gus seems distracted. Yesterday after training he left straight away with a group of other boys rather than staying to train with me like he usually does. I should probably bring it up with him and make sure he's okay.

⚽ ⚽ ⚽

The next day as training finishes, I spot Gus making a beeline for the exit and quickly run over to him to catch up before he leaves.

"Of course I'm fine bro, why wouldn't I be!? We are crushing the league, and I'm having the time of my life doing it!"

Gus is happy, smiling, his usually charming and laid back self, he nudges me in the ribs. "Look you need to lighten up bro, you're easily the best player here, we all know that, but me and the lads think you need to come on a 'team bonding exercise', get to know everyone better, relax a bit you know?"

Team bonding? Gus always did have a way with words, and he knows I'm no idiot.

"So what does this *'team bonding'* usually involve Gus?"

"You know, having a laugh, staying out late, meeting new people…dancing…see where the night goes…you know…*fun*!"

Gus certainly seems happy, and relaxed at the moment, but I can't shake the feeling that his performances have been slightly below par recently. Perhaps it's to do with all this partying after training?

On the other hand, I have been feeling a bit of an outsider recently and the idea of having some fun, letting my hair down and hanging out with my teammates does sound really appealing. Why shouldn't I enjoy myself? After all, like Gus says, I'm easily the best player here so I don't really need to worry about my performances.

Would one night out hurt that much?

DECISION TIME

To relax a little and go out with Gus and your teammates, go to page 60

To stay at training practicing free kicks, and turn Gus down, go to page 12

CHAPTER 45

I SHOUTED AT WIGHT, "BACK POST, NOW!" AND wrapped my foot around the ball to give it enough curl to direct itself into his path. The Lilywhites defense could only watch as the ball sailed over their heads and onto Wight, who guided the ball goal-bound with his forehead.

It was at moments like these when everything moved in slo-mo. Their goalkeeper desperately scrambled across the goal line as the ball rifled off the post and down into the empty net. My teammates rushed to Wight and me to celebrate the goal. The fans jumped out of the red seats to embrace each other.

I was already off running toward the supporters. Jumping into the celebrating fans. WOW.

WE WERE AHEAD. 2-1. The league was ours!

I took a quick glance over at Sir Alec on the touchline. He raised a thumb and then mouthed, "not a shot though was it son." He had a point.

One trophy down, TWO TO GO.

Go to page 62

CHAPTER 46

I WAS FURIOUS. THIS WASN'T THE TIME TO ATTACK everyone. We had played well since the goal and were in a great position with 45 minutes to go.

"Yes boss, I do." I said, standing up from my seat. "You've torn three of us apart in front of our teammates, killing our confidence with the biggest 45 minutes of our careers ahead. What kind of management is that?!"

The words came out before I could catch them and now they charged at Sir Alec, like a Spanish matador waving a red cape at an angry bull.

"You what lad? Who tha' hell do ya' think you are'? Ya' wee cocky one..."

Sir Alec lurched forward and shoved me in the chest.

I stumbled backwards and hit the floor in a state of shock and pain. I had let anger fill the room and we were all now feeling the consequences. Sir Alec looked at me in a haze of anger and regret.

He shouted at his physio. "Get him checked now." Sir Alec stared at me on the ground for a beat and then grabbed the substitute midfielder David Grey; "Chuck ya' jersey on son, ya' playin..."

There was a knock on the door, the officials letting us know we were needed on the field.

The lads left the room with the manager and his coaching staff.

I began taking my cleats off, as the realization of what had happened took hold. I wasn't going to get to play in the rest of this Champions League final or a Manchester Devils soccer jersey again.

I hadn't realized Beano was standing by the door. "Wow. That did not go well, did it, mate?!" His attempt at humor was appreciated but falling on deaf ears in my current mood.

"Get yourself cleaned up." He put his hand on my shoulder, gave it a quick supportive squeeze and left the locker room.

I wasn't sure I wanted to play for Sir Alec again and was fairly sure I wouldn't.

We lost the final and missed a once-in-a-lifetime chance to win a treble.

Sir Alec didn't talk to me after the game and I quickly found out from my agent that Manchester Devils were looking to sell me in the summer.

After the news came out about what happened, there was a lot of support for me and the way I had been treated by Sir Alec. I was so pleased.

Manchester Devils put me on the transfer list and I was approached by two clubs.

. . .

DECISION TIME

If you choose to move to Westfalen in Germany, go to page 189

If you choose to move to FC Catalonia, go to page 136

CHAPTER 47

To Daveed's surprise, instead of passing it back to him, I let a thunderbolt of a strike loose into the London Blues net. My coaches had always told me to be confident and take a chance when I felt instinctively that there was a goal to be had, and I'd done just that! My teammates grabbed me and dragged me over to our fans, who were spilling out onto the field in pure joy and excitement.

The referee blows for full-time. We won 2-1 and I'd helped bring a long overdue trophy to the London Lilywhites!

As we're walking up to collect our trophies, Daveed calls my name, giving me a momentary look of anger before breaking into a laugh and handing me his cleats, "you earned this today l'enfant. Two goals in a final? Tre bon." He patted me on the shoulder. "Swoosh will be calling you tomorrow."

Go to page 5

CHAPTER 48

As I put the ball down, I see Peter, our goalkeeper, arrive in the box. It's all or nothing time.

I whip the ball toward the center spot, straight at Peter who can leap like a salmon. He just misses it, but it lands behind him and is cleared to the edge of the box. Riggsy hits it straight back in, hoping for someone, *anyone*, to knock it goal-bound.

Teddingham is first to react, getting there before the Monchen defenders. He pivots and lashes the ball into the bottom left corner of the German goal. WE'VE ONLY GONE AND EQUALIZED!

Teddingham runs at me, followed by a swarm of cheering Manchester players. Riggsy climbing over Teddy, screaming in joy at our fans who are celebrating in front of us.

I grab Teddingham by the jersey. "We've got this. We're going to win it. Right now, not in extra-time. NOW."

Teddy turns and shares my message, it spreads amongst the team like wildfire.

Belief. It can be so contagious.

Go to page 44

CHAPTER 49

I'm woken up in the middle of the night by a weird noise. Curiosity gets the better of me and I make my way across the hall to my dad's room.

He's on the phone to my mom. It turns out that weird noise was actually Dad sobbing. I had never seen him cry, so the sound of him sobbing down the phone really gets to me.

"I miss you and my daughter so much. It feels unnatural not being around my whole family. I can't wait to be in your arms." He says to Mom.

Wow. This was making me feel so bad. Nothing was more important in life than family. Not even soccer.

"I don't know when I'll see you next, darling. It *really* is up to him."

"Let's make it tomorrow, Dad." I burst into the room and give him a huge hug to cheer him up.

"Let's go home. Let's reunite the family. It's been eight months and I still haven't played for the first team. Enough is enough. I can make it big back home."

Two years after I came back from Europe and reunited my family, the Jewels Old Boys manager called me in. I still remember the conversation as if it was yesterday:

"Listen kiddo, I'm not going to beat around the bush," he said, as I sheepishly sat down at the other end of his desk.

"It's been two years since you've been here and you haven't progressed. I hate to say this to you, but you're too short to ever play this game professionally. We're going to release you from your contract."

I remember he kept waffling on, but I was in shock. I couldn't stop his words from echoing in my head. "Too short to *ever* play professionally."

Jewels Old Boys never funded my growth hormone treatment and everyone outgrew me.

From a soccer perspective, my heart broke. But at least I had brought my family back together which made me happy.

AND JUST LIKE THAT, MY SOCCER CAREER ENDED.

CHAPTER 50

GAME DAY. WE NEEDED THREE POINTS AGAINST Gunnerbury to beat them to top spot and win the league. WINNING the English league in my first season at Manchester. It's what dreams are made of.

I stared down at my breakfast, moving the eggs around the plate instead of eating them. I was too excited and too nervous to eat. My phone buzzed. It was a text from Renato Conaldo.

> THREE POINTS. THAT'S ALL WE NEED AMIGO. EAT YOUR EGGS.

I sometimes had to pinch myself that I was friends with him. That he would be calling me, passing to me on the field and celebrating goals together. My sister was SO jealous.

I knocked back my eggs in double time, eager to get to the training ground for the team bus to the stadium. The Theatre of Dreams. My dream.

We could hear the fans from the locker room. They were in full voice today. Nothing gave you more extra energy than when our fans were on our side. I always acknowledged them whenever I was lucky enough to hear my name from the stands. I had a habit of waving, which they loved and laughed at in equal measure.

BANG. BANG. BANG. Beano was kicking a soccer ball against the wall. He did this before games to rev himself up. He screamed louder with each kick too; knowing that Gunnerbury's players were on the other side of the wall. He was by far the scariest player I'd met in the sport. On my first training session for the club, he scissor-chopped me down from behind because I had tried to nutmeg him. I never tried that again.

The door swung open and in marched Sir Alec, the manager. His determination to win manifesting itself in how red his face got before games. Today it was a deep claret.

"Lads, these wee cabbages next door don't know what's about to hit 'em." He punched his fist into his hand, looking at each of us in the eye, before punching it again. "Aye, they play some good soccer, but they cannae take a challenge and they cannae defend crosses."

Beano then charged at the magnetic whiteboard, flying into it with a diving header. He skidded through it, sending the tactics flying. "Come on lads. COME ON! I want to see each and every one of you leaving it all on the field today." He said, picking himself up from the floor. "Three points. The league title. It's that simple."

Sir Alec smiled like a proud father. This was the attitude he loved.

Renato Conaldo walked past me, winking and laughing it all off. "You got this amigo. Cross that ball, I'll get on it. Just like we do every day at training." He fist-bumped Beano and walked out the room.

The boss started toward me. "Start aggressively. End aggressively. Ya 'noo you can beat that wee kid on the wing." He patted me on the shoulder. "That goal you and Renato scored in training. I want tha'. I want tha' on repeat. I want tha' spread on ma' toast every morning."

He chuckled as he stalked off through the door toward the field and dugout. I gave myself a moment as I stared at the number 10 jersey hanging in front of me. I can do this. I've got this.

⚽ ⚽ ⚽

Gunnerbury were taking no prisoners today. Every crunching tackle we did, they came back with two. I had four stud marks on my thigh to prove it.

We were 2-1 down after 30 minutes and the rain was pelting us in the face sideways. My mom would call this biblical, but I preferred to call it British.

Tooney called my name from the frontline. "Wake up mate. Stop the day-dreaming. The manager is watching you!" I glanced over. He was. The color in his face now a deep purple.

I needed to up my game and I needed to do it NOW.

Our goalkeeper kicked the ball long and high toward me. Here was my chance.

As the ball made its descent to me, I saw the Gunnerbury midfielder ready to make a challenge through the back of me.

When the ball hit the ground, I immediately changed the direction of it with a Cruyff turn; sending him skidding on the grass, as I gracefully carried the ball forward. I heard Renato laugh and clap, before the fans erupted and started singing my name.

There was a bit of an issue in that the infamously nasty Gunnerbury French defensive midfielder Piera was coming for me like a missile shot from a submarine. As skillful as he was aggressive, I knew I needed to move the ball on quickly or I'd have a few more stud marks on my thighs before too long.

Paul Skols, our attacking center midfielder, called for the ball. I curled a pass 20 yards ahead of me to his feet and continued my run beyond the angry Frenchman. Paul saw me and knew what I had in mind. I was just on the far right edge of the box when I met his pass back to me, and immediately started running toward the by-line. When I got there, I could hear Renato Conaldo desperately shouting my name. He was unmarked in the box.

DECISION TIME

If you cross the ball to the back post, go to page 126

If you cross the ball to the penalty spot, go to page 72

CHAPTER 51

"Do you even know *anything* about soccer?!" I shout in my manager's face.

"Because you seemed like a clueless idiot out there! Why didn't you bring me on? Could you *NOT* hear all the fans chanting my name?!" A red mist had descended over me, it really *was* uncontrollable.

Before I knew it, I was shoving my manager in the chest.

He stumbled backwards and fell on the ground, I could see in his eyes that he was very angry too. He dusted himself off and, like a deranged bull, stared at me for a second that seemed a lifetime.

"Who do you think you are, you spoiled little brat?!" He spat as he started charging towards me.

I clenched my fists, prepared to feel the full force of his impact on my body, but it wasn't long before a dozen or so of my teammates and backroom staff got in between us both. They separated us and the assistant manager took me straight to the team bus.

"Take him home and come back for us in an hour," were his instructions to the bus driver.

It was when I got to the team hotel and turned on the TV that I saw the live press conference my manager was giving about me.

"It's safe to say he got too big for his cleats. We've sent him home." The national manager said.

"What lessons do you think he should take from this?" Asked a reporter from across the room.

"That soccer is a team sport. No player will *ever* be greater than the team he plays for. Not Marantini, not Lelé, not him".

He seemed a lot calmer now than he did an hour ago.

So was I. I knew then and I know now that violence is never the way. I just don't know what came over me.

"He is the most talented youngster I have ever seen." The manager continued at his press conference. "But unfortunately, you need a good attitude and a good work ethic to make it big in this sport."

"It's unfortunate that after his behavior today, he won't be playing for the national team again".

It was whilst sitting in that hotel room, ironically still in my national team's uniform, that I learned that I would never again play for my country. My club also cancelled my contract after my outburst.

AND JUST LIKE THAT MY SOCCER CAREER ENDED.

CHAPTER 52

"No mate, you've got this. You're the best in the world!" It was just what he needed to hear.

As I got into the box, I turned to see Peter, our goalkeeper, arrive too. It was all or nothing time.

Beckenham whipped the ball toward the center spot, straight at Peter who can leap like a salmon. He just misses it, and it lands behind him as it's cleared to the edge of the box. Riggsy hits it straight back in, hoping for someone, *anyone*, to knock it goal-bound.

Luckily, I'm first to react, before the Monchen defenders, pivoting and lashing the ball into the bottom left corner of the German goal.

I SCORE. WE EQUALIZE. THE PLACE GOES MAD.

I run at Beckenham, followed by a swarm of cheering Manchester players. Riggsy climbing over me, screaming in joy at our fans who are celebrating in front of us.

I grab Beckenham by the jersey. "We've got this. We're going to win it. Right now, not in extra-time. NOW."

Beckenham turns and shares my message, it spreads amongst the team like wildfire. Belief. It can be so contagious.

Go to page 44

CHAPTER 53

When I made the decision to stay at Jewels Old Boys I did it only with my mom and dad's best interests at heart.

I knew I was a good player and could make it in Spain, but it just wasn't worth risking all of my parents' savings without even knowing if I'd get a trial at the world's greatest soccer club.

The thing is, it's now been two years and I really haven't grown at all! All the teammates that I was with two years ago are now playing with the first team. I can still easily get past anyone in the youth team, but it's when I play against adults that they easily outmuscle me and outplay me.

The physicality of it all has really nestled in the forefront of my mind, and that's why I'm extremely nervous that the manager has called to see me into his office. Especially today of all days, the last day of the regular season!

"Listen kiddo, I'm not going to beat around the bush," he says, as I sheepishly sit down at the other end of his desk.

"It's been two years since you've been here and you haven't progressed. I hate to say this to you, but you're too short to ever play this game professionally. We're going to release you from your contract as of today..."

He keeps waffling on, but I'm in shock. I can't stop his words from echoing in my head. "Too short to *ever* play professionally."

My heart breaks.

AND JUST LIKE THAT MY SOCCER CAREER ENDED.

CHAPTER 54

I REGRET NOTHING. THESE PAST FEW YEARS AT Manchester Devils have been glorious.

We managed to retain the league title the following season as well as a bunch of Cups and League Cups along the way.

Sir Alec announced his retirement last season after beating London Blues in a Champions League final - leaving this great club in the hands of his successor. It's been a tough change but with the new guy in charge and a few older faces still in the squad, I believe this historic club will be fine.

There's a bit more gray in my hair than before and my sprints aren't quite as fast as they once were, but I always remember the words of my coach as a kid – be patient, watch the game.

It's served me well.

We go into the World Club Cup Finals against Mexican side Talum FC off the back of a four game winning streak in the league. The manager rested me over the weekend, so I'm ready to go.

The final is taking place in the capital city of my home country.

I haven't played for my country for a while now, for reasons that are slightly beyond me. The eccentric manager Dogo Armenio Marantini has ideas of his own!

As I walk out into the stadium for the final, the reaction of the fans is incredible.

The game is tough and hot, but I'm loving it.

Despite Talum FC's energy and resilience, they can't get near us and I feel like my younger self.

Stepping out of first gear in the second half, the match starts to take shape. Our talisman, Wes Tooney, bags himself two lovely goals, much to the joy of our fans and me. I assisted both.

With confidence pulsing through my bones and wanting to give the home fans something to remember, I pick the ball up in midfield and run toward goal. I bob and weave between the Talum midfielders, nutmegging their center back as the goalkeeper closes the space between us. I step over the ball, making the keeper shift his weight onto his wrong foot, whilst knocking the ball the opposite way and sliding it into the goal.

3-0, one of the greatest goals of my career, and a World Club Cup to take home to Manchester.

Perfect.

A strange thing has happened.

My performance in the World Club Cup caught

the eye of my home country's press, who are calling for my immediate international call-up.

The national team are struggling in their World Cup qualification. After a bad run of results in the group stage, they need a win in the final match against top of the table Chile. Win and go to the World Cup; lose and face public embarrassment at home. It would be the first time the country hadn't made a World Cup in 50 years.

My phone rang in my pocket. RING. RING. RING.

I didn't recognize the number but it was a dial code from my home country.

I hear Marantini's gruff voice down the end of the line. "Look, I don't want you in my team but the other players and the press do." He wasn't making this easy.

"We have one game against Chile to win and we go to the World Cup. You won't start, but you'll be on the bench ready if I feel like I need you."

I laughed to myself. Quite the invite. "Okay, I will do this for my country and my family. See you soon."

And just like that I flew back to my home country again!

Everything has been off since I arrived.

I haven't seen a team or locker room so divided before. For all of Marantini's former success and skill as a player, he really wasn't a man manager.

I sat quietly in my warm substitute jumper at half-time, whilst the players and manager argued over whose fault a misplaced pass was.

Marantini shouted for quiet. "You guys don't know what you're doing. Soccer is easy. This country is steeped in soccer folklore, we should be beating teams like Chile."

I shared a look with a fellow substitute, another player who had fallen out of favor with Marantini.

"NO CHANGES. GET OUT THERE AND SHOW ME SOMETHING."

Despite it being 0-0 and our attackers having no shots on target for a full 45 minutes, the manager wasn't going to put players on he didn't like.

The second half was more of the same. Chile closed off the space, aggressively knocking our players about and keeping a solid shape. The match needed fresh legs.

Marantini finally made some substitutions with 15 minutes left, but I didn't get the call.

It was then that I heard the crowd. They were singing my name. Marantini looked at me, looked at the crowd and then shook his head.

Things got worse. We gave away a silly penalty.

As the Chilean player stepped up to the ball, you could feel the tension. Marantini was standing at the edge of his technical area, hands clenched in hope and anger.

OVER THE BAR. A massive let off for us...but how long would that last?

A Chilean player threw himself into a challenge, studs up, catching Angel in his thigh. His cries were loud and painful, even from my seat, 50 yards away on the subs bench.

And then I heard it again. The crowd were singing my name once more. Louder and more intensely.

I saw the physio tell the manager Angel was done. This was it, Marantini had no other attacking midfielders – he had to send me on.

"Okay, get out there and impress me. Personally, I've never seen it in you, but good luck!"

That was all the encouragement I needed. I took my jumper off, checked Angel was Okay as he was stretchered off, and determinedly jogged onto the field. The crowd was excited and so was I.

I was welcomed to the field with a hard shove from a Chilean midfielder. Nothing I hadn't experienced before. They'd need to try harder.

I was happy with my first touches; receiving the ball around the edge of the Chilean box, prying for space and a chance to shoot. I just needed our strikers to make a run, which they weren't. Great.

There was a series of angry boos as the fourth official signaled that there were just two minutes left.

If I was going to do something, I was going to have to do it quickly.

Linking up with our midfield, we drew the Chilean midfielders out with a series of neat passes, before executing a one-two between their lines to release me into their box. WHACK.

My legs were swept from behind me. The whistle blew for a free kick, 25 yards out.

I picked myself up, dusting off the mud from my knees. I was tapped on my shoulder and handed the ball by a young striker. "It's all yours." He jogged away, laying the foundations for me to change the fortunes of our national team.

I placed the ball down. Looking up to assess my options from this distance. I knew I could hit the target, but it would have to be one hell of a shot. A less greedy player would curl one to the back post, hoping our strikers had enough about them to pile on the pressure and knock it home.

DECISION TIME

If you choose to cross the ball to the back post, go to page 130

If you choose to take a shot, go to page 49

CHAPTER 55

IT WAS HALF-TIME IN THE CONTINENTAL CUP FINAL against Brazil, and we were 2-0 down. As I walked down the tunnel, I was angry.

Soccer is a physical game, I knew that, but the number of times I had been fouled today was starting to hurt. "Keep drawing the fouls. The ref is going to start booking them soon," said our attacking coach, putting his arm around my shoulders for support.

The door opened, and in walked the manager. He made a beeline right for me; this didn't look good. "I have just come from the referee's room. He has told me that if you don't stop diving, he will send you off." I was dumbstruck.

"Diving? I've been kicked all half, look!" I said, pointing to six fresh stud marks on my calf under torn socks. "I can't believe this idiot thinks I'd dive." I was angry again.

"Guys, it's 2-0, but all to play for. Stay on your feet and be braver," the manager bellowed this across the locker room, but I knew it was directed at me. "COME ON, LET'S DO THIS!"

I had always been taught that if you got angry, you should close your eyes, count to 10, and relax. Right then, I was finding this very difficult.

Peeeeeeeeep. The referee blew to start the second half.

This Brazilian side was truly brilliant. Strength, skill, confidence, and ball retention... they had it all. Although I was taught to save my energy, not chase the ball, and read the game as it happened, this side was starting to undo everything I had ever learned in my soccer career.

A long ball was kicked up to me from our goalkeeper, it was high and flat, coming at me at pace. I knew what was going to happen, so I braced myself for the knee in the back from a Brazilian. BANG.

As I collapsed onto the ground in pain, the Brazilian smirked and ran on. Fully expecting a whistle from the referee, I stayed on the ground... but it never came. Instead, the referee in his black jersey, shorts, and socks strutted up to me and said, "One more, and you're going in the book."

The crowd erupted in a cacophony of boos. It was impossible to know if they were against me or the ref, but the red mist rose behind my eyes, ready to blow.

A teammate picked me up and whispered, "you better be careful now, bro." Why couldn't anyone see that I wasn't doing anything to cause this?!

I dusted myself off and jogged back into position. Right, that's it. If I couldn't beat them physically, I was going to have to do it skillfully.

The Brazilians were complacent in possession for the first-time all game and passed the ball to our right wing back. I was already bursting with pace toward the edge of Brazil's box, so he slotted a quick ball into my feet, knowing I was ready to wind my way through their defense.

The Brazilian player who had just put me on my backside hurtled my way, his intentions clear. With the goal in sight, I wound my foot back like a slingshot, ready to dummy and delicately dink it into the net. But a hand tore me from my feet and onto the ground.

The whistle blew. A penalty, surely. A goal is a goal. Good.

When I looked up, the referee was pointing in the other direction. He'd given a foul against me. A FOUL. And to compound my anger, I watched him reach into his pocket and raise a yellow card at me.

That was my limit. I rushed toward the official, exploding in a fit of anger. I was blocked by teammates, they were pulling me back, trying to stop the oncoming trouble I was about to start.

I could hear my teammate in my ear. "Calm down, calm down. He'll send you off. We need you."

DECISION TIME

If you stop, allowing your teammate to speak to you, go to Page 90

If you shrug him off, knocking him off his feet and then go on to argue with the referee, go to page 67

CHAPTER 56

"I'M SO GLAD I NEVER WENT TO SEE THOSE SCOUTS," I think to myself as I sit in the dugout next to the manager.

We are playing our local rivals Spanijol, and 99,000 fans have packed our stadium to produce one of the best atmospheres I have ever seen!

"*This* is what I stayed for," I mumble to myself as I scan the stadium banners and see the confetti rain onto the field. We're leading Spanijol two goals to nil going into the 80th minute. The win is in the bag and our fans know it!

It was the day after those scouts tried to tempt away from FC Catalonia, that the manager invited me to train with the first team. I think I've been doing alright the last two weeks, but the manager still only ever puts me on the bench. In fairness to him, we've got Brazilian superstar Bobaldinho playing in my preferred position, and he happens to be having his best season ever, so I can't be too upset.

It's just so frustrating to be sitting in front of

99,000 adoring fans instead of *playing* in front of 99,000 adoring fans.

The clock ticks into the 82nd minute and I find myself trying to work out the wording on one of the banners in the crowd. It's got Bobaldinho in the center and some words underneath that I can't quite work out… "OI! DAYDREAMER!"

The manager shouts at me and I immediately snap out of trying to decipher the banner.

"Do your stretches. You're going on!"

Butterflies invade my stomach. I'm feeling so excited that I feel like I'm going to throw up!

As I start my stretching I have to suppress a little tear, this really is the proudest moment of my life. All the sacrifices my mom and sister made, the hard work my dad put in for me, all those years of missing my family and friends back home. It was all for this one moment. To play for the first team of FC Catalonia.

As the flurry of thoughts continue occupying my head, I find myself high-fiving the legendary Portuguese midfielder Decu on the sideline as I come onto the field to replace him.

Still a teenager, I have become the youngest player ever to play for FC Catalonia, and I'm not gonna lie. This feels good. This feels *very* good.

Go to page 21

CHAPTER 57

I KNEW I COULDN'T JUST SIT THERE AND SAY NOTHING while they laughed at me, or they would have been laughing at me all season - there was only one way to deal with bullies, and that was by standing up to them!

I turned to them standing, and although I was only short, I did my best to look big and imposing. I opened my mouth, stuttering momentarily, "Was... was something funny to you two?! Where exactly would you like me to sit - I have to sit somewhere, don't I?!"

Zhivec approached me. To say he towered above me was an understatement. He was HUGE! He was topless, with his muscles bulging and his long hair in a tight ponytail. He stared at me, saying nothing, and made me feel as small as I had ever felt. I could feel myself going red as the locker room slowly filled up with the rest of the team. He addressed the room like a seasoned politician:

"Has everyone here met our newest recruit? He's

a smurf-sized nobody from the backwaters of who knows where."

There was a smattering of laughter from the players as Zhivec continued, "This player here, this little smurf .....sorry, what is your name boy? I'm not sure I've heard it before?"

Again, more laughter...

I went to answer, but he carried on; the question was clearly not meant to be answered. "This player here, is supposed to be the heir to the great Ratan Zhivec, but he can't even find where he is supposed to put his bottom, so I don't know how he expects to be able to find the goal."

There was more laughter, more players now filling up the locker room. He looked at me and winked as I turned a deeper shade of red, embarrassed and unable to come back. Luckily for my dignity, the manager entered the locker room and told everyone to head out for training.

⚽⚽⚽

I felt angry as we headed out for training and tried to suppress the feeling. I always played with a smile on my face, but it wasn't going to be easy with someone like Zhivec embarrassing me like that. I had always been quite a shy boy and had always found soccer to be a great leveler. If you were good enough, you were good enough - everything else was just noise. Still, I couldn't help but feel angry, and the more I tried to suppress it, the more agitated I began to feel.

Training got underway with some of the most intense physical exercise I'd ever experienced, lap after lap of running and short sprints finished with a long-distance run and a beep test. A beep test was where you ran between two cones at ever-decreasing time intervals which were marked by a beep. If you didn't make it between the cones in time, you dropped out until only one player was left, and that player would be proclaimed as the winner. No prizes for guessing that for the last three years, Zhivec had been the winner of this pre-season ritual.

The test got underway, and before long, there were only a few of us left: Zhivec, the captain Ruiz, my roommate Sanchez, and me. As the intervals sped up, I found myself tiring, but I knew I had plenty of energy left. I used to get my dad to time and shout the beeps for me back home in my garden and would practice this drill over and over.

As Sanchez and then Ruiz dropped out, I started feeling confident; my lungs weren't burning yet, and it was just me and Zhivec. I could see him tiring as we raced between the cones, so I gave him a smile and couldn't help myself from saying, "You're looking tired there, old man. Are you sure you don't need a rest?"

He snorted in retort, and we were off again, racing between the cones. I could see him breathing heavily now, struggling as I pulled ahead, waiting for him at the cone before setting off again on the next beep. Every time he came in after me, I encouraged him sarcastically. "Nearly there, old man." "Are you okay? You don't look it." "You can quit now if you want?"

Before long, he tired and dropped out, and I was crowned the winner to a smattering of applause. I turned to Zhivec with a smile and a shrug as I was embraced by some of the younger players and patted on the back by Sanchez. Zhivec brushed past me and muttered menacingly, "You will regret that, little smurf."

I immediately regretted what I had done; being smug and arrogant wasn't who I was at all. Why had I acted like that? Why had I let my anger get the better of me?

The session ended with some small-sided games. We then played in a reduced sized field with small goals and no goalkeepers, which was designed to put an emphasis on close control and one-twos. I received the ball from my teammate and, with the coach watching on, I glided past two experienced players before sliding the ball to Sanchez to tap into the goal. We kicked off again, and again I beat two players before this time slotting the ball into the goal myself. As I jogged back, I felt a hard shoulder charge into my back, sending me crashing to the floor. I knew it was Zhivec, but I didn't turn around. I looked up toward the coach, but he was now watching one of the other small-sided games. We were clearly left to referee this game ourselves.

A few minutes later I got a pass from my teammate. When I received the ball, I beat one player, beat two, pirouetted around the stretching Ruiz, before looking up to see Sanchez running through on goal. As I went to slide the ball through to him, I felt two feet slide in hard from behind, taking me out. I screamed out in pain and looked down at my leg; part of it was pointing in the wrong direction. It was broken in two places!

As I lay on the floor in agony, I just had time to catch the silhouette of a tall, ponytailed man jogging off with the ball before I suddenly got an almighty feeling of regret. I should not have antagonized him so much throughout my first training session. I passed out and was rushed to the hospital with a broken leg.

AND JUST LIKE THAT MY SOCCER CAREER ENDED.

CHAPTER 58

I TOLD MY MANAGER ABOUT THE NIGGLE AND HE SENT me straight to the Club Doctor:

"Son, you are INCREDIBLY lucky that you've come to see me today," he said.

"I've rarely seen a hamstring this badly torn. If you'd have played one more game of soccer I'm confident that you would have snapped it completely and ended your career there and then!"

WOW. I was in shock! I had been very close to ending my career. Luckily, by listening to my body, it gave me the chance to make a full recovery.

⚽⚽⚽

The injury did mean sitting out for a few months and watching my teammates win the European Champions League without me, which was devastating. But what it also meant, was that I came in fresh and injury-free for the upcoming World Cup.

That is, of course, if the national team manager selected me to be in the squad.

Go to page 25

CHAPTER 59

As I stepped off the plane, the first thing I felt was rain. Cold wet rain running down my arms.

I turned to the gray sky. Welcome to summer in England.

As my parents couldn't join me in England immediately, I was met at the airport by the London Lilywhites youth team coach, Jamie. He was holding a sign that read 'Future G.O.A.T.', with a crude drawing of the animal below it. I liked him immediately.

"Hey mate…or all hail the special one, should I say." Jamie slapped me on the back and took me into his embrace. "Sorry mate, I'm a hugger." He looked down at me. "You are NOT dressed for this country."

Rain squelched in my flip flops. He was right.

"No worries my new friend. There's full training gear waiting for you at the training ground." He ushered me to follow him. "Off we pop. Time to make a soccer player out of ya'."

It had only been a few days since I'd met the

agent for Lilywhites, but I already had a good feeling about this change!

⚽ ⚽ ⚽

The next nine months were some of the best but hardest of my life. The training was like nothing I'd experienced – blood, sweat, and tears...but not necessarily in that order. Some sick too.

But I was feeling stronger, faster and fitter every day that went by.

London Lilywhites are a historic team fighting in the top half of the Premier League and the fans are incredible. After my first appearance for the club – a 7-0 win against Berkshire FC in the FA Cup – they created a song about me. I remember hearing it carry around the stadium when I was on the field and it's all I hear in the street now.

The manager is great. 'Arry' or 'Gaffer', as he likes to be known, encourages me to be brave and attack. "None of this defend from the front nonsense with you son," he says with a chuckle. "You watch the game, save your energy n' pounce when you get the chance."

We are having a pretty good season by all accounts. We don't have the cash that the big clubs do; so I'm not yet playing alongside the best in the world, but I am sharing the locker room with some incredible internationals and a couple of club legends.

The captain, Dedley Ling, looks out for me on the field and is no push over. It's good to feel your team have your back, especially when I'm a few years younger than everyone. I've seen my fair share of half-time tunnel arguments where my teammates have had a thing or two to say about an opposition player trying to remove my legs with a studs up tackle. I even saw someone throw a pizza once.

After a hard-fought semi-final against a club called Birmingham Bandits from the midlands, we're in our first final for a decade! The prestigious League Cup at the famous Werberly Stadium against one of our biggest rivals – London Blues.

The gaffer likes to play the younger players in the Cup competitions so I have played every one of our four games to get to the final and am guaranteed a start.

I'd begun to build a bit of rapport with the silky French winger Daveed. Our playing styles complement each other. So much so that I'd managed to get two assists for him in the semi-final.

He said if he scored a hat-trick, his cleats were mine.

I am a bit of a match day soccer boot hoarder. Most people have wardrobes full of their own clothes, but mine is spilling out with the cleats of some of the best players playing in the English league right now.

It's good to have a hobby, my mom always said.

⚽ ⚽ ⚽

It's League Cup Final day and I am STOKED.

We're sat in the massive Werberly locker room and I'm reminding myself of how lucky I am to be here. Amongst my teammates are French World Cup winners, a four time FISA 'Best Player in The World' nominee, two German European Championship winners, three Team GB Olympic Gold Medallists and a French catwalk model/international soccer star… that's the famous Daveed. My dad didn't like how much my mom liked him!

He caught me looking at his cleats. I blushed and turned away, hoping he wasn't still looking at me. "'Ey l'enfant, you lookin' at me or tha' cleats?" His famously bright pink swoosh tick soccer cleats sat proudly on a shelf above him. "They are very bright." I replied.

"If a defender iz looking at my cleats, they r' not lookin' at the ball." He joked. I turned around and put my Lilywhites jersey on. I wore number 18 – iconic at the club due to a former German striker, Jamie had told me the day I joined.

Tap. Tap. Someone was tapping me on the back. I turned around to see Daveed smiling at me. "I tell you what; if you assist me AND score today, I will do two things. Un, I will give you 'dis pair for your collection. Deux, I will get you your own contract with Swoosh. Deal l'enfant?"

I laughed. He didn't. He was being serious.

"Er, yeah, okay. I'll see what I can do Daveed." I replied, a little wary of what I was promising and fully aware of the kicking I was about to get on the field today. London Blue's center back, Jay Perry, was a renowned bully. A great player, but a bully.

"Challenge set l'enfant." He jogged off through the doors to the tunnel. I turned back to the locker room to see Dedley, our captain smiling at me.

"He won't forget that. He is 100% serious. If you get the chance to set him up today, do it!"

I nodded. Winning the League Cup AND a new boot contract with Swoosh? I was ready.

It felt like we had had four seasons in one match.

What started as warm sunshine and a smooth, dry field to play soccer on, quickly turned into a bit of a mud fight when the heavens opened. The grass was slick and the ball was wet – The Soccer Gods were not smiling down on us today.

0-0 and half-time had rolled by with not much to report on. London Blues were tough, tight and ruthless given the chance. Our star midfielder, Aaron Manderton, was the target of many of the London Blues tackles – his legs catching feet, shins, knees and studs like a human magnet.

'Arry refused to play it safe and kept encouraging us to push forward and "give 'em hell." It felt a bit like they had the same plan.

On 70 minutes, disaster struck. Our French goalkeeper Hugo placed a stray pass into the feet of London Blue's prolific goal-scoring attacking midfielder Tampard, who took two touches and struck a deflected shot off our captain, into the bottom corner.

One nil down, 20 minutes to go and more rain on the field than in the ocean.

The gaffer made two quick subs, pulling off a striker and a right midfielder who were clearly exhausted. Ling walked over before we kicked off and passed me a note from the manager. It read:

"I DON'T PAY YOU TO GET WET. DO SOMETHING."

He had a point and by bringing on an extra player in midfield, he gave me the space to push into the hole behind the strikers. Finally. It was my time to try something.

The next 10 minutes were all a bit of a blur. I began receiving more of the ball, much to the joy of the London Lilywhites fans who had started to sing my song - acting like 40,000 conductors, controlling what we were doing on the field.

I took a great pass from Daveed, through the lines of their pressing center midfielders, giving me 10 yards of space to burst into. Our striker was screaming for the ball to be passed to his feet on the edge of the box, but he hadn't realized that his run had opened up a gap. I had.

I knocked the ball in front of myself and ran into the box, the goal leering up at me to my left. I could see the London Blues goalkeeper, trying to make the angle narrow but it was too late. I knew where I wanted to put it. I pulled back my foot like a pinball machine and let fly.

It skidded up off the turf and into the far-left corner, but was blocked by Perry with his hand, which was up in the air, desperate to stop the ball any way he could.

The whistle blew. PENALTY.

Daveed cooly picked up the ball and placed it on the spot. The jeers and boos from behind the goal rose up like a wave of distraction.

Daveed took one step back and slowly put his foot through the ball to the right corner. As sweetly as he hit it, I could tell it was a little too wide. He was going to miss this.

I stepped forward, a second before everyone else, and moved to the goal, pre-empting it hitting the post. IT DID and was coming straight at me. I positioned myself in a split second and threw my head toward the ball, hoping I'd judged it right to save Daveed's mistake.

The ball pinged off my head and flew back toward the goal, the London Blues goalkeeper jumping limply from the ground after diving for the penalty but missing it entirely, as it hit the roof of the net.

GOAL. 1-1.

A header? I don't score headers!

Before I could get up the whole team was on me. A pile of players in white jerseys. Daveed pulled me up. Gave me a fist bump and said, "Damn. Merci l'enfant."

Spurred on by our good fortune, we piled on the pressure. London Blues were getting more and more annoyed with every decision so had started making mistakes.

The rain had stopped and a small burst of sunshine shot across the field for the final few minutes. As much as I had got used to this country's weather, I was hugely appreciative of a dry spell.

But it certainly wasn't a dry spell on the field.

To compound Perry's miserable day, he was sent off for a very late challenge on Daveed. Down to 10 men and with a very clear goal-scoring chance for us, everything felt set to win this League Cup.

Something that Daveed and I were good at were effective one-twos that dragged players out of position quickly, giving either player the space to shoot.

As though telepathically, he looked up with the ball at his feet as I moved into position. He lined up to shoot, acting with all intention to put his laces through the ball for a shot. He took a long run up to really sell the dummy and then slotted a pass to his left and into my path in the box. As the London Blues team all turn their attention to me, I wind my leg back and…

DECISION TIME

If you dummy a shot back into the path of Daveed, go to page 53

If you go for glory and take a quick shot before London Blues have had time to close you down, go to page 148

CHAPTER 60

It's been a whirlwind, signing terms, saying goodbye to my teammates and finally arriving for my medical in Germany. I was in great shape, so I flew through my medical. I was now joining up with the first team well in time for pre-season training.

I was put into a house with another new arrival and fellow countryman, Esteban Sanchez, who'd recently signed from FC Riveria - the idea being that having someone who spoke the same language would help me settle into my new surroundings. We'd be studying German together and had a staff member assigned to us for our wellbeing. The club was really going out of its way to look after me.

In front of me in the team's pecking order was the club's best player: Ratan Zhivec. The imperious Swedish international and the team's main goal threat. His contract was up at the end of the season and the rumors were that he'd already agreed a deal behind the scenes to join Milano.

If I played well and was patient, perhaps I could be taking Zhivec's place in the team next year. In fact, my agent had been told as much when we were negotiating the contract. I was apparently being signed as Zhivec's long-term replacement. He'd averaged a goal every one and half games in the last three seasons. I had big shoes to fill - the gigantic Swede standing at 6"4.

Go to page 70

ABOUT THE AUTHORS

Michael Langdon is an accomplished writer and a seasoned attendee of five World Cups, showcasing his deep-rooted passion for soccer. He embarked on his soccer journey by coaching youth soccer in the United States, laying the foundation for his future endeavors.

He has faithfully followed his beloved England team at the past five World Cups and regularly indulges in Saturday afternoons at The Amex stadium in Sussex, watching Brighton & Hove Albion exceed expectations.

⚽⚽⚽

Dan Clark is a trained journalist and photographer who now runs his own creative business from his base in Dorset, England. He loves long walks, storytelling and following his soccer club Reading FC (although he often wishes he didn't). He's also a LA Rams and Denver Nuggets fan but will pretty much watch any sport, anytime, with anyone.

His first book, 'Be The Goat - A Pick Your Own Soccer Destiny Story' was written in collaboration with Michael Langdon and Matt Hamm and allows young readers to choose a path through a soccer career from young soccer fan to becoming the world's best player.

Matt Hamm is a trained journalist and multi award-winning marketing manager. Sadly as a fan of Tottenham Hotspur, that's where the winning ends.

Matt is based in Anerley, London and is a lover of all things soccer. He is a season ticket holder at Selhurst Park, the home of the Premier League's Crystal Palace.

His first book, 'Be The G.O.A.T. - A Pick Your Own Soccer Destiny Story' was written in collaboration with Michael Langdon and Daniel Clark. The story allows young readers to choose a path through a soccer career from youth academy to becoming the world's best player.

Printed in Great Britain
by Amazon

51421427R00116